meat, game & poultry
cookbook

Consultant editor
Sarah Banbery

Love Food ® is an imprint of Parragon Books Ltd

Parragon
Queen Street House
4 Queen Street
Bath BA1 1HE, UK

ISBN: 978-1-4075-5455-6

Printed in China

Created and produced by
The Bridgewater Book Company Ltd

Commissioned photography Clive Bozzard-Hill
Home economist Sandra Baddeley
Illustrations Coral Mula

The Bridgewater Book Company would like to thank the
following for permission to reproduce copyright material:
Getty Images, title page; Franken/Corbis, page 11; George
D. Lepp/Corbis, page 22; and Murat Taner/zefa/Corbis,
page 23.

Notes for the Reader
This book uses imperial and metric measurements.
Follow the same units of measurement throughout; do
not mix imperial and metric. All spoon measurements
are level: teaspoons are assumed to be 5 ml, and
tablespoons are assumed to be 15 ml. Unless otherwise
stated, milk is assumed to be full fat, eggs and individual
vegetables are medium and pepper is freshly ground
black pepper. Recipes using raw or very lightly cooked
eggs should be avoided by infants, the elderly, pregnant
women, convalescents and anyone suffering from an
illness. Pregnant and breastfeeding women are advised
to avoid eating peanuts and peanut products.

CONTENTS

INTRODUCTION

The *Meat, Game and Poultry Cookbook* is a comprehensive guide to choosing, buying, storing and cooking meat, whether it be red meat, poultry or game. If you find yourself struggling to identify the bewildering variety of cuts of meat available, or perhaps you want to know the best way to cook different types of poultry, then here you will find all the information you need in a single volume. From finding new uses for familiar meats to preparing more unusual and hard-to-find game, this book will give you not only the confidence to select the appropriate and best produce, but also a wealth of both traditional and contemporary ways to cook and serve it, drawn from culinary traditions across the globe.

INTRODUCTION

There are many kinds of meat, and different cultures may favour or avoid eating certain species, but in the Western world, 'meat' means common farmed or wild mammals and birds. The majority of us are meat-eaters, but often look no further than a packet of mince or the Sunday roast to satisfy our appetites and tastebuds. This book aims to inject a new spirit of excitement into your kitchen by helping you to explore the myriad tastes and textures of various types of meat, to make your meat cooking more creative, adventurous and delicious.

Eating meat may not, strictly speaking, be essential for our survival but it is nutritionally important and tastes good. The huge variety of recipes in this book demonstrates meat's versatility and popularity throughout the world as the basis for nutritious, delicious meals for the whole family. For those who may be less experienced with the whole topic of meat, it might be a good idea to read through this chapter before you start choosing which recipe to try first. It will give you guidance on selecting and storing the most common types, whether they be red meat, poultry or game. There is also a section on how to prepare for cooking what you have chosen, details on all of the essential cooking techniques and advice on the best carving techniques.

This book will also help you to identify good meat. Where possible try to buy the best produce that is on offer and don't be tempted to go for poor-quality meat. It is far better to buy smaller amounts or cheaper cuts of good meat rather than large amounts of bad. Not only will you see the benefits in the nutritional value of the product, the difference in taste between is considerable – once you have developed a taste for good, fresh meat, you'll never want to eat poor-quality meat again!

CHOOSING MEAT, POULTRY AND GAME

To take advantage of the huge variety of meat, poultry and game available, including cured, preserved and processed meats as well as offal, it is useful to have a basic understanding of what is on offer in its various forms.

MEAT

Terms applied to different varieties of a particular meat, such as lamb, are often related to the age of the animal. It is worth bearing in mind that the meat of younger animals is generally more tender, but also less pronounced in flavour, while older animals are likely to be tougher yet tastier.

BEEF AND VEAL

Beef is the meat provided by domestic cattle, while veal is the meat of the young calf. Beef usually comes from castrated male cattle slaughtered at between 18 and 24 months and veal from male calves slaughtered at either three weeks, 18–20 weeks or between five and six months. There are many types of beef produced from a large number of different types of cattle, including: 'dairy cross' meat from the offspring of a dairy cow and a bull, 'prime beef' from a pedigree herd, 'rare' beef from breeds such as Aberdeen Angus, or prized 'kobe beef', which comes from Wagyu cattle.

HALAL AND KOSHER MEAT AND POULTRY

These types of meat and poultry are raised according to religious law and ritually slaughtered by a specialist butcher with a razor-sharp knife. They are available from specialist butchers and some supermarkets.

LAMB AND MUTTON

Lamb is the meat from a young sheep, and there are several types.

Baby lamb/suckling: milk-fed lamb no older than ten weeks and weighing less than 9.1 kg/20 lb.

Spring lamb: several months old and 9.1–18 kg/20–40 lb.

Lamb: five months to one year old and most commonly available.

Hogget/yearling: meat from a lamb that is one to two years old.

Mutton: meat of a mature sheep over two years old.

PORK, HAM AND BACON

Pork is the fresh meat of the domesticated pig. Traditionally, pork was seasonal meat, much of which was salted and preserved to provide ham, bacon and sausages. Most pork is slaughtered between six and nine months old, and anything older is termed a 'hog'. 'Rare-breed' pork is almost exclusively free-range.

OFFAL

The term 'offal' derives from 'off-all' and refers to the edible parts of an animal left when the meat is removed from the carcass. This includes organs such as heart, liver and kidneys as well as tongue, brain, thymus gland (sweetbreads), stomach lining (tripe) and blood (used in black or blood pudding). Offal also covers pig's feet/trotters, head and cheek, ox tail and calf's foot.

POULTRY

Poultry is defined as domestic fowl bred specifically for eating. Raised for their meat and eggs, poultry includes chicken, turkey, duck, goose and guinea fowl.

CHICKEN

Chicken is the most popular and widely available form of poultry. It is sold under a number of different names according to its age, size and method of rearing. The following are the most common types of chicken you are likely to come across:

Poussin: an immature chicken, four to six weeks old, weighing up to 450 g/1 lb with delicate, moist meat.

Spring chicken: a small, young bird weighing up to 1.15 kg/2 lb 8 oz.

Broiler or roasting chicken: the most common bird for roasting, a full-sized bird weighs between 1.3–2.7 kg/3–6 lb.

Boiling fowl: an older bird, usually a laying hen weighing 2.7 kg/6 lb.

Capon: a castrated young chicken bred for its tender, white flesh.

Corn fed: chickens fed on corn, which produces a yellow flesh and skin with a flavour comparable to guinea fowl.

Free range: indicates that a limited number of birds are housed per square metre/yard and have outside access for at least half their life.

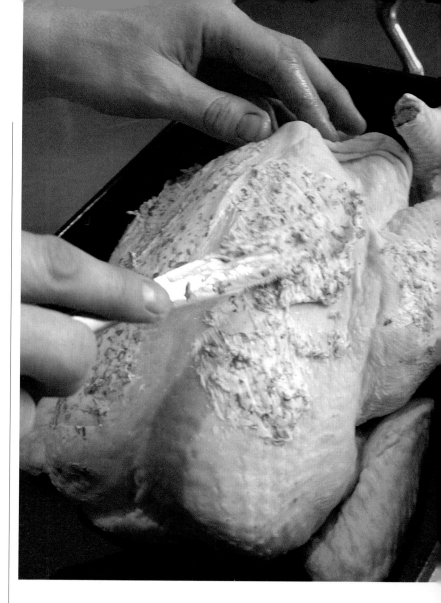

Traditional free range: indicates chickens that have more space and must have had outside access from the age of six weeks.

Free range–total freedom: is very similar to traditional free range, except that during daylight hours, outside access is unrestricted.

Battery: intensively reared chickens with no outside access, killed at six weeks old.

Organic: chickens raised with a regulated standard of welfare, that are GM-free and have been fed with antibiotic-free food and with guaranteed access to forage and feed outside.

GUINEA FOWL

Originally game birds, guinea fowl are now almost exclusively farmed. Slightly smaller than chickens when plucked, guinea fowl are sold as squabs weighing 550 g/1 lb 4 oz, chicks weighing up to 1 kg/2 lb 4 oz or fowls weighing up to 1.7 kg/3 lb 12 oz. The hen bird is considered to be the more tender.

TURKEY

Descended from the North American wild turkey, this domesticated bird is available all year round. A young turkey weighing 3.6–11 kg/8–24 lb will provide about 70 per cent white meat and 30 per cent dark meat. Allow an average of 350 g/12 oz per person. The rearing methods for turkeys are similar to chickens, so an organic, free-range bird will have a better flavour and texture than an intensively raised bird.

READY-PREPARED CHICKEN CUTS

You can purchase chicken in a variety of forms to save on preparation time, including: chicken quarters; part-boned or boneless breast; drumsticks (legs); thighs and wings.

DUCK AND GOOSE

Duck is a waterfowl, now mainly raised commercially and widely available. There are a number of varieties, and as with all poultry, a younger, free-range bird will taste better than an older, farmed bird. Most duck on offer is actually duckling, which is six to eight weeks old, but duck up to 16 weeks old is sometimes sold. A 2.7-kg/6-lb duck will feed two or three people.

Goose is a large water bird popular for roasting and raised free-range. Fatty and with rich meat, it has an average weight of 2.7–5.4 kg/6–12 lb, but because of its meat to fat ratio, a goose will only feed four people, on average.

GAME

Strictly speaking, 'game' is defined as birds and mammals that are wild and hunted for the table. Traditionally, game has been a seasonal food, usually available for a short period of time, and from wild animals and birds shot for the pot and sold through a game dealer. However, today very little game is truly wild, and it is available for most of the year. Farmed, frozen or imported game birds and animals may well have lived part of their life 'wild', but have nevertheless been reared specifically for supplying to supermarkets and butchers. More unusual game is now available by mail order from specialist game dealers. It is useful when buying game birds to know if they are young birds, which will roast well, or older birds that will need to be braised or stewed for the best results. Game is traditionally 'hung' to develop flavour.

PHEASANT

The pheasant is a long-tailed game bird originally from China and related to the chicken, available farmed or as wild game birds. Traditionally, a 'brace', or a male and female pair of birds, is cooked at one time, the smaller hen bird being regarded as the most juicy and tender. Pheasant tend to be very lean with a strong, rich flavour and are best enjoyed roasted or braised. Wild birds are in season from October to February, but fresh, farmed birds are available generally from September to March. One pheasant will feed two people. Keep refrigerated for two days – any longer and the birds will acquire a very strong 'gamey' smell and taste.

GROUSE

Grouse are a family of sought-after wild game birds, which includes the sage grouse, capercaillie and the red grouse. Fairly lean and with a distinctive flavour, the grouse is only found wild. A good bird can be distinguished by its plump breast and unblemished skin. Older birds should be casseroled or braised rather than roasted. Available from August/September, one bird is usually served per person and they can be hung for up to ten days, depending on how strong a flavour you desire.

PARTRIDGE

A small, plump, flavoursome game bird, the best-known partridge are the red-legged and the grey-legged. Farmed partridge tend to have less

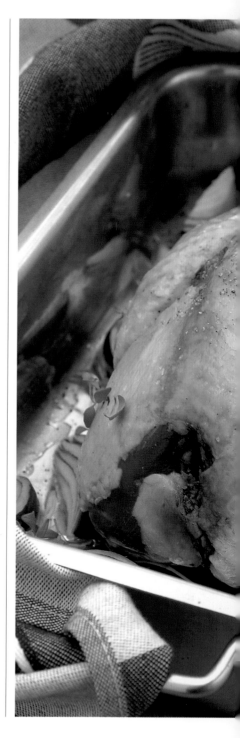

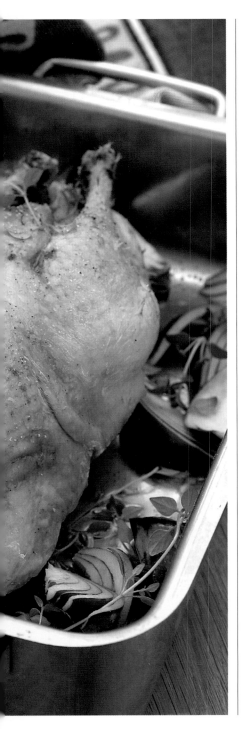

taste than their wild counterparts, but the meat of both is very lean and highly flavoured. Related to the pheasant, partridge have a slightly firmer flesh and should be prepared and cooked in a similar way. One bird is usually served per person.

QUAIL

A small game bird related to the pheasant and partridge, quail are available almost exclusively farmed. The quail has a pink, moist flesh when cooked, and due to its limited size, it is usual to serve two per person as a main dish. Available all year round, the quail is also prized for its tiny eggs, traditionally used in canapés. Often prepared part-boned for stuffing, quail can also be spatchcocked.

WOODCOCK AND SNIPE

Both woodcock and snipe are rare and highly prized wild birds, sought after for their dark, intense meat. As they are difficult to shoot, they are not generally available, although they can occasionally be acquired from a good game dealer or direct from a shoot. They do not generally improve with age, so should be cooked within a week of obtaining them. Traditionally, the woodcock, and sometimes snipe, are cooked whole (with their intestines), including the head. Allow one bird per person.

PIGEON AND SQUAB

Pigeon are common game birds and there are hundreds of species worldwide. A squab is a young, domesticated pigeon that has never flown. Pigeon flesh is dark, rich and dense, with very firm flesh on the breast, while squab tends to be more succulent and pink. Widely available, pigeon is best cooked as fresh as possible and the breasts are often shallow-fried or roasted; older birds require slow cooking.

MALLARD, TEAL AND WIDGEON

These birds are types of wild duck. Mallard are also raised semi-wild specifically for shooting, so tend to be more widely available. Mallard have lean, dry flesh and should only be hung for one day. One bird will serve two people. Teal and widgeon are almost exclusively wild and therefore more flavoursome, with a rich, strong-flavoured flesh, and tend to be smaller than mallard. Serve one bird per person.

VENISON

Venison is defined as 'large antlered game' and therefore, as well as deer, it includes elk, caribou, moose, antelope, bison and buffalo. Venison is still mainly sourced from deer, and until farmed venison became widely available, it was seasonal, expensive meat. Venison is lean, close-textured, dark, moist meat, with a pronounced gamey flavour. All venison animals are similar in taste and texture, and the same cooking methods apply. The best deer venison comes from a young buck deer aged up to two years. Broadly, the meat can be treated in the same way as beef, although it is leaner and therefore often needs the addition of pork fat to keep it moist. Prime roasting joints tend to come from the leg (haunch), the loin and the saddle, while the fillet or boned loin provides steaks. Much of the rest of the meat can be used in different ways, including being casseroled, made into sausages or minced.

HANGING MEAT

Hanging a carcass or part of a carcass, literally from a hook, ages or matures it. The process allows the muscle to relax and tenderize, and to lose moisture, which means that the meat is less likely to shrink or dry out when cooking. All meat should be hung for a few days, and mature beef, mutton, venison and other game benefit from longer hanging to allow the flavour to develop.

RABBIT

Available both farmed and wild, rabbit is an inexpensive, low-fat meat. Wild rabbit is considered to have a more pronounced flavour than farmed. Rabbit meat is pale and fine-grained with a delicate flavour, and although available year round, the 'season' for the best-quality rabbit is August to February. Rabbit is usually eaten at three months old, and one rabbit will feed two people.

HARE

Larger than a rabbit, with long back legs, the hare is almost exclusively available from game dealers. The meat is rich, moist and with a distinctive flavour. As with other game, young hare is best roasted or 'jugged' – marinated, casseroled with vegetables and served in a sauce enriched with the hare's blood and liver, and cream. Older hare should be casseroled or only the saddle roasted. One hare should feed two or three people.

WILD BOAR

A traditional European game animal, the wild boar is a wild pig that has distinctive dark, rich, close-grained meat, which contains much less fat than domestic pork. Until recently almost exclusively wild meat, boar are now being farm-raised and have increased in popularity for 'hog roasts' and boar sausages. Boar is butchered in the same manner as pork and the most tender cuts come from the loin. Boar should always be cooked well done.

BACON AND GAMMON

This is cured back and belly pork. Gammon comes from the hind leg of the pig. Bacon and gammon can be either wet-cured in salted water or dry-cured, where salt or a mixture of salt, sugar and spices are rubbed into the pork. The meat can then be smoked.

HAM

The hind leg of the pig is, similarly to gammon, salted and air-dried or brined and smoked to make ham. There are a number of curing methods that involve a variety of seasonings, spices and sugar, and may include such flavourings as molasses, beer and red wine.

SALT BEEF

Dry-cured brisket or silverside beef is known as salt beef. The longer the meat spends in the salt or brine defines how salty the final meat will taste, and the longer it is cured, the longer it will last, but it may well have to be soaked before cooking.

AIR-DRIED MEATS

Air-drying is a further maturing process for cured meat – once cured, the meat is hung and left to dry and develop further. Most air-dried meats, including air-dried sausage

SALAMIS

These air-dried, cured sausages use natural casings made from preserved and reconstituted animal intestines, which are pliable for stuffing with meat.

CURED, PRESERVED AND PROCESSED MEATS

'Curing' simply means preserving by various age-old methods of salting, pickling, air-drying, wind-drying and smoking or otherwise treating meat and offal to ensure that it will last longer than fresh meat. Processed meats include pâtés, terrines, potted meats and pies.

(salami) and Parma and serrano ham, are then eaten raw.

COLD-SMOKED MEATS

Cold-smoking is another method of preserving and flavouring meat, once again applied to ready-cured meat. The meat is hung over smoking coals or woodchips, which further reduces the moisture content of the meat and adds preservatives. Most cold-smoked meat needs cooking.

CONFIT

In this method of preserving, the meat is initially dry-salted – sometimes spiced – and then cooked for a long time in rendered fat until very soft, poured into a jar and completely covered in liquid fat, which solidifies and preserves the meat for up to six months. This is a popular method for preserving duck, goose, rabbit and pork.

SAUSAGES

Fresh sausages are made by blending lean, chopped meat and fat with seasoning and spices, herbs and cereal or rusk. Most meat, game and poultry are now available in sausages, including duck, venison and wild boar. The meat content of sausages varies greatly and there are some varieties of sausage, such as black or blood sausage, that are made without meat. The best sausages have a high meat content with a good amount of pork fat to keep them moist, with well-balanced flavourings and natural casings. Good sausages should not be pricked before cooking, as this leaches out the fat that keeps them moist.

PIES

Pork or other pork-based picnic pies, including game pie, are really terrines, where pastry replaces the dish. The pastry surrounding the chopped meat should be a lard-rich, hot watercrust pastry and the pie should keep fresh for up to a month. Other raised pies include veal and ham, poultry and pork, and game.

PÂTÉS AND TERRINES

Pâté is distinct from a terrine in that terrines tend to have larger pieces of meat and/or vegetable, whereas a pâté is either a smooth paste or has a coarse chopped-meat texture. Liver is often the basis of a pâté (pork or chicken), with the addition of chopped pork. Goose liver pâté is the most luxurious. Game also works well in pâtés and terrines because of its strong, distinctive flavours. Both pâtés and terrines are a traditional way of using up left-over meat or offal and can be made of virtually any pieces of meat, poultry or game, including sweetbreads.

BUYING MEAT, POULTRY AND GAME

Nowadays there are various ways in which you can buy meat, poultry and game, and where you buy your meat can affect not only what you buy in terms of availability but also quality. As well as being discriminating as to sourcing your produce, it is well worth learning how to detect the signs of well-produced and processed meat, poultry and game. While it is unnecessary to know every cut of meat and where it comes from, it is useful to understand broadly what you need to buy for the intended purpose and the end result you want.

WHERE TO BUY

The usual sources include supermarkets, butchers, markets, farm shops and producers, a game supplier or straight from the wild. Many people are becoming more interested in where their meat comes from and will spend time sourcing meat from a particular supplier to satisfy their own concerns regarding welfare and nutrition.

SUPERMARKETS

A majority of the meat we buy still comes from supermarkets and they have the advantage of huge buying power. They also offer convenience both in terms of long opening hours and ready-prepared produce, as well as a guarantee of freshness. The labelling of supermarket goods gives the consumer some information on sourcing of products, and in recent years more effort has been made to raise the standards of animal welfare.

GAME SUPPLIERS AND WILD SOURCES

Many game birds and animals are now available from supermarkets and specialist butchers, but traditionally, it was the game suppliers who provided wild game shot by a local shoot. This is still the case, and buying game through a traditional supplier is the only way of guaranteeing freshness and indeed having the opportunity to hang your own game and prepare it at home.

THE INTERNET

Meat is increasingly available by mail order from suppliers via the Internet and many supermarkets now provide shopping on-line for home delivery. The Internet is also a good way of investigating farmers' markets and local producers. Rare or unusual meat, such as ostrich and buffalo, can usually be sourced from specialist suppliers and there is also information on offer regarding animal welfare and organic standards, as well as recipes.

BUTCHERS

A good local butcher should offer a wide choice and be knowledgeable with regard to the provenance of the produce, be able to order and prepare special cuts of meat for you and generally offer reliable advice when you are making a purchase. You are also likely to find the more traditional and unusual cuts of meat and game from a butcher. He or she should also know how long meat or game has been hung.

MARKETS, FARM SHOPS AND DIRECT SALES FROM PRODUCERS

Those who are concerned with animal welfare and traceability will more often source meat, poultry and game direct from producers or via a market or farm shop. Dealing direct with the producer means that the consumer can be satisfied as to the way in which the meat has been raised, transported and slaughtered.

WHAT TO LOOK FOR

Once you begin to understand what to look for when choosing meat, poultry or game, the whole process of cooking becomes easier, as you are likely to have selected the best-quality meat for your dish.

BEEF AND VEAL

Avoid bright pink/cerise meat with very little fat, as this indicates that the meat has not been properly hung and is likely to lack flavour – well-hung beef will have a deep colour and flavour. Good-quality beef should be deep red, dry and with a sheen (not wet or sweating), and slightly tacky to the touch. The meat should be open-grained, have good marbling (see opposite) and a significant amount of creamy fat – the fat should not be yellow or grey and any beef with a pink/brown two-toned colour or unpleasant smell should be avoided. Veal should be a delicate pale pink colour with very little fat.

LAMB

The flesh should be light red in colour, moist and with a layer of firm, creamy fat. A good-quality lamb joint should have fresh, plump flesh, a significant layer of fat and pliable skin. Avoid any lamb with yellowing fat or greying flesh that has a strong smell.

PORK

The flesh should be pale pink, smooth and fine-grained, with a visible moist sheen, while the fat should be creamy, pale, firm and with a pliable, smooth rind. The rind is a good indicator of freshness and should be thin, pinkish and flexible. Avoid any pork with a rubbery, thick or brown rind with any hair.

CHICKEN AND TURKEY

Birds should have plump breasts, white flesh under unblemished skin and the legs should be pliable with taut skin. The skin should be a pale white/cream and the bird should not be wet or leaking blood. Corn-fed chicken will have a yellow flesh and skin.

DUCK AND GOOSE

Duck has darker meat than chicken and a greater proportion of fat. Look out for long, plump breasts with unblemished skin – the skin should be pale, creamy and dry. The legs should be flexible with a good layer of fat under the skin. Like duck, goose should be plump, with a good fatty layer and pale, unblemished skin.

GUINEA FOWL

Guinea fowl should look like a cross between a chicken and a pheasant, with a plump breast and creamy, dry skin.

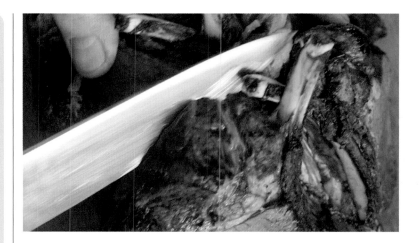

CHOOSING CHECKPOINTS

When making your selection of produce, you should carry out the following checks:

- Meat should not be wet or flabby: it should be shiny, firm and tacky to the touch. Avoid meat swimming in blood or bloody water.

- Take a sniff: fresh meat and poultry does not smell strongly, and only well-hung meat or game should have a distinctive 'gamey' smell.

- Chicken should be pale and supple: avoid any chicken with stained skin or dryness around the edges.

- Check the colour of fat on meat: it should be opaque and creamy. Avoid any fat that is yellow or brown.

- Look for good marbling in joints of meat (see below right).

GAME BIRDS

If you can obtain game birds unplucked, it is easier to establish their freshness. A soft, flexible bill and claws indicate a young bird, while a harder, less-flexible bill and ragged claws are the features of an older bird. It is more difficult to establish freshness if you have an oven-ready bird, but in general, a soft, flexible breastbone and plump breast indicates a youngster. Game birds should be hung, but an overpoweringly 'gamey' smell may indicate a bird that is past its best. Because game is hung intact, unlike beef and lamb, temperature has a crucial effect on how long the bird should be hung, and this really is a case of following your nose – the stronger the smell, the stronger the bird will taste.

VENISON AND WILD BOAR

Venison meat should have a dark, burgundy red appearance with very little fat. Moist and close-textured, it should be firm to the touch, lean and juicy. Wild boar also has dark meat, but resembles pork more closely but with less fat. Boar has dense, close-textured meat.

RABBIT AND HARE

They should be well covered in flesh, with a rounded back. The flesh should be pale pink, dry and with a sheen. Pure white fat should be present around the kidneys.

MARBLING IN MEAT

'Marbling' is a reliable indicator of the quality of meat. Marbling is the term for the network of fine fat threaded throughout the flesh, which melts and bastes the meat as it cooks, keeping it moist and tender. It is most obvious in beef, but can also be detected in pork and mutton.

CHOOSING THE RIGHT CUT

It really is essential that you choose and buy the appropriate piece of meat for a particular cooking method. Even the cheapest cut of meat, such as a beef skirt or oxtail, will benefit from the right treatment – marinating and then slow cooking is a foolproof way of dealing with what might otherwise be a tough piece of meat. Always check the recipe or with your supplier that you are using the right cut of meat – if in doubt, always order the cut or bird you need in advance. You can usually arrange for your meat or bird to be prepared ready for your dish if you plan ahead. Don't feel you have to struggle to de-bone or otherwise prepare your meat when a butcher can usually do all the hard work for you.

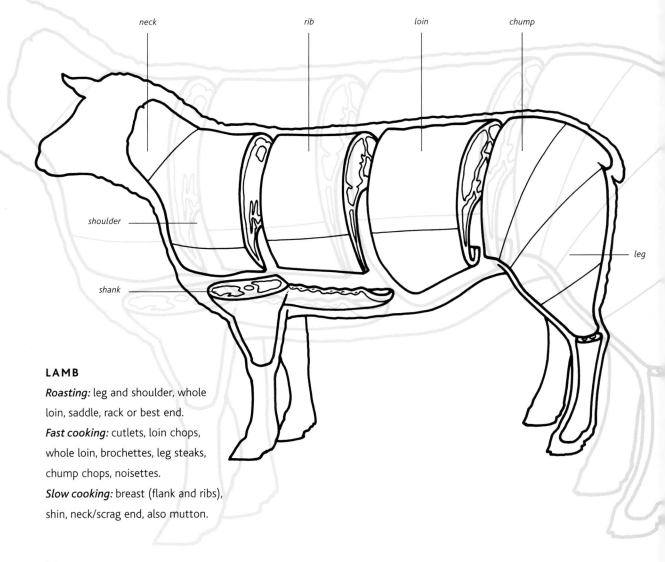

neck   rib   loin   chump

shoulder

shank

leg

LAMB
Roasting: leg and shoulder, whole loin, saddle, rack or best end.
Fast cooking: cutlets, loin chops, whole loin, brochettes, leg steaks, chump chops, noisettes.
Slow cooking: breast (flank and ribs), shin, neck/scrag end, also mutton.

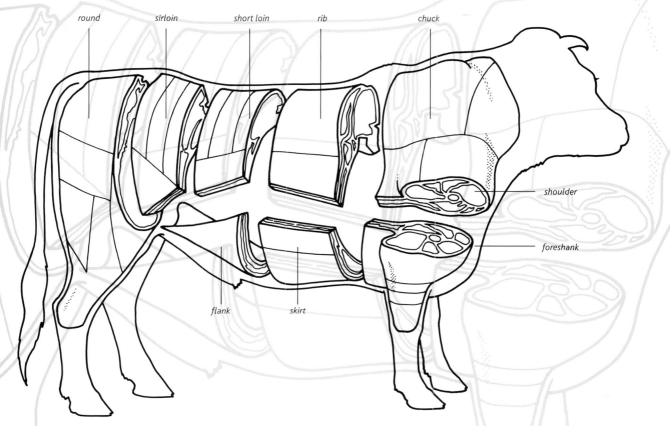

round · sirloin · short loin · rib · chuck

shoulder

foreshank

flank · skirt

BEEF

Roasting: sirloin joint, double-rib joint, wing rib, back rib.

Fast cooking: prime beef steak, fillet or tenderloin (filet mignon/ tournedos), sirloin steak, rump steak, T-bone steak, rib-eye steak.

Slow cooking: forequarter meat, such as chuck or blade, shoulder steak, skirt, top rump, topside, oxtail and rump/leg or hock, shin, silverside, topside, short ribs, brisket.

VEAL

Roasting: topside (cushion), loin, chump end or fillet roast, shoulder.

Fast cooking: escalopes, veal chops.

Slow cooking: breast (flank and ribs), shin, neck/scrag end.

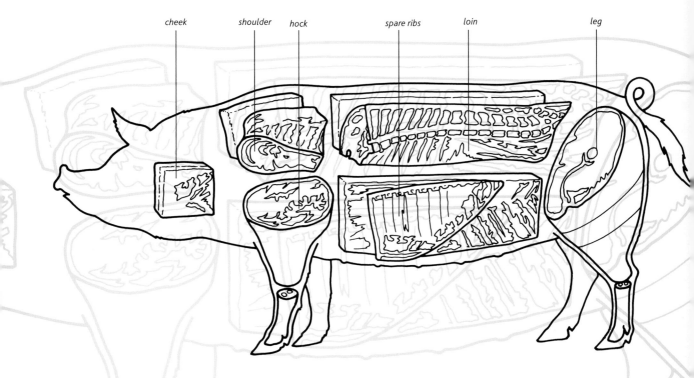

cheek   shoulder   hock   spare ribs   loin   leg

PORK

Roasting: leg, loin or spare-rib, tenderloin, belly.

Fast cooking: fillet or tenderloin, chops, escalopes, leg steaks, bacon.

Slow cooking: bacon joint, gammon, shoulder, knuckle of bacon.

POULTRY

Roasting: chicken, duck, goose, turkey, guinea fowl.

Fast cooking: chicken breasts.

GAME

Roasting: young game birds, venison (saddle and leg), young rabbit.

Fast cooking: venison steaks, pigeon breasts, pheasant breasts.

Slow cooking: older game birds, venison, rabbit and hare.

STORING AND HANDLING MEAT, POULTRY AND GAME

It is vitally important to store and handle meat, poultry and game safely to prevent any bacteria that may be present from spreading and causing food poisoning.

HANDLING

• Always wash your hands after handling raw meat, poultry or game.
• Thoroughly clean all boards, utensils, surfaces and knives with boiling water when they have been in contact with raw or thawed meat.
• Keep a separate chopping board for preparing meat and poultry, and make sure that it is always scrupulously clean.

STORING

Be sure to follow these guidelines to ensure a high standard of food hygiene and safety:
• Store raw meat or poultry in clean, sealed containers on the bottom shelf of the refrigerator, so that it cannot touch or drip onto other food.
• Follow any storage instructions on labels and do not exceed the 'use by' date.
• Store cooked meat in the refrigerator or freezer as soon as it has cooled. Always keep cooked meat and raw meat separately.
• Larger game or turkey can be kept outside, well wrapped in a secure place, with the temperature not exceeding 8°C/46°F.
• Vacuum packing is not good for meat, as it tends to make it sweat, so remove any produce from the pack and either store in a sealed container in the refrigerator or put onto a plate covered with a clean tea towel in the refrigerator.

• Do not keep fresh meat for longer than two days.
• Fresh meat mince and offal should be used on the day of purchase where possible.

FREEZING

It is safe to freeze raw meat, poultry and game as long as you follow these guidelines:
• Freeze any meat before its 'use by' date.
• Follow any freezing and thawing instructions on the label.
• Thaw in a microwave only when the meat is to be cooked straight away, otherwise leave in the refrigerator until thoroughly thawed.
• Use thawed meat within two days of thawing.
• Always cook thawed produce thoroughly and until piping hot.
• Raw meat that has been thawed and cooked may then be re-frozen, but only once.
• Liquid can appear when meat is thawing and this must not come into contact with other food, so keep in a sealed container and drain regularly.
• Poultry must be thoroughly thawed, but never attempt to speed up the thawing process by using hot water.

FREEZING GAME BIRDS

If you wish to freeze game, make sure it is hung to your satisfaction and plucked, drawn and ready to cook. Wipe any excess blood from the carcass. Wrap it in paper, put in a freezer bag, seal and freeze. Thaw thoroughly and cook as usual, bearing in mind that the freezing process may render the flesh slightly drier than that of a fresh bird. Frozen game can also be cubed and frozen, then thawed for making a game casserole or pie.

PREPARING MEAT, POULTRY AND GAME

How you prepare your produce for cooking has a major bearing on the end result. There are various ways in which you can enhance its flavour and ensure succulence. Whole chickens or turkeys are mostly sold ready prepared for roasting, usually without giblets. But you may want to divide up a whole bird into separate pieces to make it more manageable for cooking. Knowing how to bone a bird is also a useful technique.

MARINADES AND DRY RUBS

Most meat benefits from seasoning before cooking, but do not overdo the salt – it is better to add salt near the end of cooking, as it can leach juices from the meat. Garlic, herbs and flavoured butter can all enhance the taste of meat, poultry and game, and a marinade or dry rub will also add character. A marinade is simply a wet flavouring and an easy way of adding taste. It may also help to tenderize some cuts of meat and game. Avoid marinades that are excessively acidic, such as those including a high proportion of citrus juice or vinegar, and do not leave the meat, game and especially poultry in a marinade too long, otherwise the texture will be adversely affected. Marinades can also be useful in providing a sauce or gravy when cooked with the meat. It is important to use marinade ingredients that have an affinity with the meat, for instance, garlic, rosemary and red wine for lamb. Dry rubs in the form of ground spices and/or dried herbs, perhaps with the addition of crushed garlic, can be applied all over the surface of the meat, poultry and game before cooking to enhance the flavour.

LARDING AND BARDING

'Larding' is a technique of adding fat to lean joints of meat or game such as venison that have very little fat on them. It will prevent the joint from drying out during cooking, keeping it moist and tender. Pork fat is usually used, cut into thin strips or 'lardons'. Prepare the joint by making incisions in the skin and pushing in the lardons, or by using a sharp knife to make incisions through which strips of fat can be threaded, to cover the whole surface evenly. Another method is to wrap a loin completely in thin rashers of streaky bacon or pancetta and secure with string.

'Barding' is simply adding fatty bacon to baste the breast of a bird. Barding is particularly important with a big bird such as a turkey but also for many game birds, which have a tendency to dryness. To protect the breast, arrange rashers of streaky bacon over the breast, which will baste the bird during roasting. Remove 15 minutes before the end of cooking to let the breast brown.

EASY CARVING

To facilitate carving, a joint can be chined, which involves simply loosening the bone in a joint, but leaving it attached. The bone can then be easily cut away before carving. Ask your butcher or meat supplier to chine your joint when buying.

31

CUTTING AND JOINTING POULTRY AND GAME BIRDS

If you have a whole spring chicken or other small bird that you want to grill or barbecue, you may wish to halve the bird. Simply lay it on its back and cut lengthways with a sharp knife or poultry shears, cutting down and through the breastbone and then the backbone. To quarter your bird, place the blade of your knife under the leg joint and cut it away from the wing, holding the knife at a 45-degree angle. You will need a sharp, heavy knife for jointing or boning, and poultry shears are also useful.

To joint a chicken and other birds into 8–10 pieces:

1 Put the bird breast upwards onto a chopping board. Pull each leg away from the body and slice through the skin and flesh until your knife hits the thigh joint. Push down firmly and twist to break the joint. Cut through the sinews and remaining skin to detach the leg from the body.

2 Cut through the joint to divide the leg into two to give a drumstick and a thigh.

3 Cut each wing off the body.

4 To detach the breast, run a sharp knife along each side of the breastbone and cut away the meat from the carcass, keeping the knife blade against the rib cage as you do so. Either keep the breasts intact or cut each in half, according to your requirements.

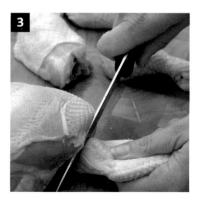

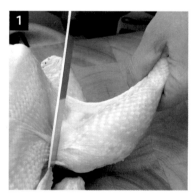

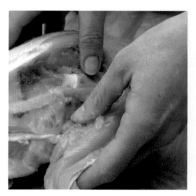

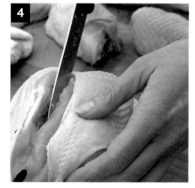

BONING POULTRY AND GAME BIRDS

To bone a chicken, duck or game bird:

1 Put the bird breast downwards onto a chopping board. Cut off the lower wings.

2 Turn the bird over and cut along each side of the breastbone and down, keeping the knife blade against the rib cage, until you reach the wing joint. Cut through the sinews.

3 Hold the wing in one hand and, using the knife, pull the meat away from the bone. Turn the wing inside out and remove the bone.

4 Cut along the side of the bird, freeing the meat, until you reach the leg joint. Cut through the sinews and, using the knife, cut the meat from the bone until you reach the next joint. Cut through the sinews and pull the bone from the flesh. Turn the leg inside out and remove the bone.

5 Cut away the rest of the meat from the rib cage along to the tip of the breastbone and the tail end, then ease out the carcass.

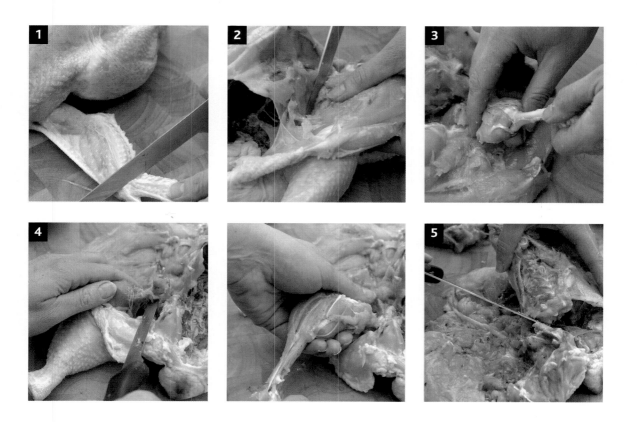

TRUSSING BIRDS

It is important to truss a bird, especially a game bird, to retain its shape during cooking, and also to keep any stuffing in place. The easiest method of trussing is to use a skewer and string.

1 Turn the bird breast downwards and fold the neck skin over the back to close the neck opening. Twist the wing tips over the skin to hold it in place.

2 Turn the bird breast upwards and, pushing the legs up towards the neck, push a skewer just below the thigh bone right through the body to emerge just below the thigh on the other side.

3 Turn the bird breast downwards again, pull a piece of string across the wing tips and secure. Loop the string under the ends of the skewer and cross the string again over the centre of the back.

4 Turn the bird breast upwards again and loop the string around the drumsticks and parson's nose. Pull the string tightly and tie the ends together.

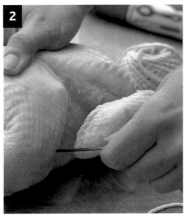

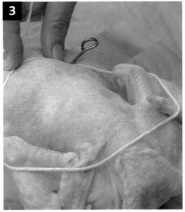

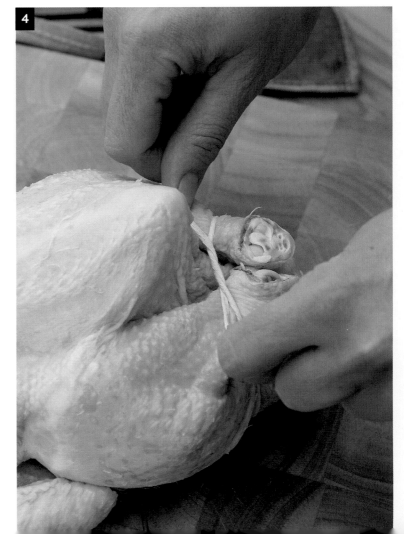

STUFFING

Suitable for both boned and rolled joints of meat, stuffing can provide extra flavour as well as help to keep the roast moist. Hearty stuffings with distinct flavours are needed to complement meat.

In the case of poultry and game, stuffing can be placed either in the neck and cavity of a bird and/or under the breast skin. Stuffing should not fill the whole cavity, or it is unlikely to cook through – the amount of time needed to cook the stuffing will most likely overcook the bird. Stuffing should not go into the bird more than an hour before cooking. Either stuff the opening of the cavity and the neck or loosen the skin between the breast meat and skin and push stuffing under the skin to cover the breast. If you are stuffing a game bird, you might consider partially cooking the stuffing before adding it, so that the bird will remain moist and not overcooked. Alternatively, cook the stuffing separately and simply put a few herbs, butter or garlic into the bird's cavity.

SPATCHCOCKING POULTRY AND GAME BIRDS

Smaller birds, such as quail and poussin, will cook more evenly and quickly when spatchcocked, or flattened, for grilling or barbecuing.

1 Put the bird breast downwards onto a chopping board. Cut through the backbone, open the bird out and press flat.

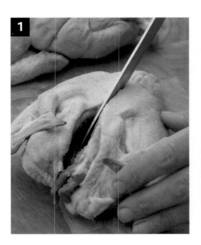

2 Insert a wooden skewer (presoaked in cold water for 30 minutes) diagonally through the body by pushing it through the thigh and out at the base of the opposite wing.

3 Repeat with a second skewer through the other thigh so that the bird is skewered flat on crossed sticks.

COOKING MEAT, POULTRY AND GAME

There are no set rules for cooking meat, as each cut requires different preparation, handling and cooking. However, generally the tender cuts are roasted, grilled or fried and the tougher cuts require pot-roasting, boiling, braising or casseroling.

ROASTING TECHNIQUES

Oven roasting is suitable for large joints of meat and whole birds. Quick roasting cooks the meat at a high temperature, which seals the meat and preserves the juices and flavour, but the meat may shrink using this method. Slow roasting cooks the meat at a low temperature over a longer period of time and prevents shrinkage. This method is more likely to produce a tender roast. Check your recipe, as this may advise sealing the meat or bird before roasting or starting the cooking for a short time at a high temperature and then reducing the heat for a longer roasting time. Baste as required during cooking.

ROASTING TIMES

Always weigh a joint or bird to calculate the cooking time. Roasting times vary according to the cut of meat or size and age of the bird, whether on or off the bone and stuffed. The times given below are guidelines only.

Generally, if meat is off the bone it will need slightly longer cooking than a joint on the bone – add ten minutes to the roasting times, and the same for stuffed, rolled joints.

ROASTING RULES

- Always preheat the oven to the correct temperature before putting in the meat or bird.

- Make sure that the joint or bird is at room temperature before roasting.

- When roasting a duck or goose, always use a rack in the roasting tin, so that you can pour off the excess fat.

- If roasting a joint or bird wrapped in foil or in a roasting bag, remember to remove the foil or bag 15 minutes before the end of the cooking time to brown.

- Always rest the meat or bird for the appropriate time, tented with foil, in a warm place.

BEEF

1 Preheat the oven to 230°C/450°F/Gas Mark 8.

2 Roast for 20 minutes, then reduce the temperature to 190°C/375°F/Gas Mark 5 and roast for:
- 15 minutes per 450 g/1 lb for rare
- 20 minutes per 450 g/1 lb for medium
- 30 minutes per 450 g/1 lb for well done.

Meat thermometer recommended internal temperature:
Rare: 60°C/140°F
Medium: 71°C/160°F
Well done: 76°C/169°F

LAMB

1 Preheat the oven to 190°C/375°F/Gas Mark 5.

2 Roast for 30 minutes per 450 g/1 lb, 30 minutes less for rare.

Meat thermometer recommended internal temperature: 82°C/180°F

PORK

1 Preheat the oven to 230°C/450°F/Gas Mark 8.

2 Roast for 25 minutes, then reduce the temperature to 190°C/375°F/Gas Mark 5 and roast for 35 minutes per 450 g/1 lb.

Meat thermometer recommended internal temperature:
Pork: 87°C/189°F
Bacon or gammon joint: 71°C/160°F

TURKEY

1 Preheat the oven to 220°C/425°F/Gas Mark 7.

2 For turkeys weighing 3.5–4.5 kg/8–10 lb, roast for 30 minutes, then reduce the temperature to 160°C/325°F/Gas Mark 3 for 2$\frac{1}{2}$–3 hours, increasing the temperature to 200°C/400°F/Gas Mark 6, uncovered, for the final 30 minutes.

For turkeys weighing 5.5–6.5 kg/12–14 lb, roast for 40 minutes, then reduce the temperature to 160°C/325°F/Gas Mark 3 for 3–3$\frac{1}{2}$ hours, increasing the temperature to 200°C/400°F/Gas Mark 6, uncovered, for the final 30 minutes.

CHICKEN

1 Preheat the oven to 190°C/375°F/Gas Mark 5.

2 Roast for 20 minutes per 1 lb/450 g, plus 20 minutes. Increase the temperature to 220°C/425°F/Gas Mark 7 for the final 15 minutes of the calculated time.

GOOSE

1 Preheat the oven to 220°C/425°F/Gas Mark 7.

2 Roast for 20 minutes, then reduce the temperature to 180°C/350°F/Gas Mark 4 and roast for 1 hour 20 minutes to 2 hours.

DUCK

1 Preheat the oven to 220°C/425°F/Gas Mark 7.

2 Roast for 20 minutes, then reduce the temperature to 180°C/350°F/Gas Mark 4 and roast for 1 hour–1 hour 10 minutes.

GAME BIRDS

Woodcock and Snipe

Roast for 15–20 minutes at 230°C/450°F/Gas Mark 8.

Pigeon

Roast for 20 minutes at 220°C/425°F/Gas Mark 7.

Teal and Widgeon

Roast for 20 minutes at 220°C/425°F/Gas Mark 7, then for 10 minutes at 180°C/350°F/Gas Mark 4.

Grouse

Roast for 20 minutes at 220°C/425°F/Gas Mark 7, then for 15 minutes at 180°C/350°F/Gas Mark 4.

Partridge

Roast for 25 minutes at 230°C/450°F/Gas Mark 8.

Pheasant

Roast for 20 minutes at 220°C/425°F/Gas Mark 7, then for 25 minutes at 180°C/350°F/Gas Mark 4.

Guinea Fowl

Roast for 20 minutes at 220°C/425°F/Gas Mark 7, then for 25 minutes at 180°C/350°F/Gas Mark 4.

GRIDDLING OR CHARGRILLING

This is another quick-cooking method suitable for the same cuts as grilling, and offers a convenient indoor alternative to barbecuing. It is also a low-fat method of cooking, as the food can be cooked without any additional oil or fat. For the best results:

• Use a ridged cast-iron griddle pan, which gives the meat attractive charred griddle lines.

• Preheat the griddle pan over a high heat until almost smoking, before adding the food and cooking briefly on either side so that it is seared and sealed.

• When cooking duck breasts, score the skin and put skin-side down into the hot pan to release the fat from the skin and keep the flesh moist while making the skin crisp. Turn and cook on the other side after about 8 minutes, depending on the thickness.

GRILLING

This quick-cooking method is suitable for small tender cuts such as steaks, cutlets, chops and chicken breasts, as well as sausages, burgers and kebabs. For the best results:

• Always brush the meat or poultry with oil, not the grill rack.

• Always preheat the grill before adding the meat.

• Do not wrap the food in foil when grilling, as this will boil it and prevent it from browning and crisping.

• Turn at least once during cooking.

• Do not cook the meat too close to the flame, or it will burn.

BROWNING MEAT

Direct contact between meat and the frying pan or grill burns the surface of the meat, creating irresistible caramelized flavours.

SHALLOW-FRYING

Shallow-frying in oil is a quick-cooking method suitable for the same cuts as grilling and griddling or chargrilling. For the best results:

• Start cooking over a high heat to seal the meat, then reduce the heat and continue to cook until tender.

• Do not overcrowd the pan, as this will boil rather than fry the meat.

DEEP-FRYING

This quick method of cooking is used for meat or poultry with a breadcrumb or batter coating, such as chicken drumsticks. For the best results:

• Make sure you have a good depth of oil and heat over a high heat to 180–190°C/350–375°F, or until a cube of bread browns in 30 seconds.

• Cook in small batches to prevent the temperature of the oil dropping and the coating becoming soggy.

• Drain the deep-fried food well on kitchen paper before serving.

BOILING

This cooking method is suitable for joints, mixed meats (as in bollito), salt beef, ham and bacon joints. Salted joints may need presoaking. The meat can be left to cool in the cooking liquid. For the best results:

• Add the meat, poultry or game and vegetables to simmering water.

• Skim regularly to remove any scum that rises to the surface.

• Keep at a regular temperature on a low simmer.

SLOW COOKING

Casseroling and braising, including ragoûts, hotpots, Carbonnade de Boeuf and Navarin of Lamb, are all methods of cooking meat slowly in the oven. Stewing, on the other hand, is a slow-cooking method for the hob, with the heat coming from underneath. These long, slow-cooking methods are suitable for tougher cuts of meat, older game birds, chicken, lamb shanks and chops. Pot-roasting is another long, slow-cooking method using a heavy, lidded pot with a small amount of liquid and vegetables. It is suitable for smaller joints or tougher cuts of meat and older game birds or chicken. Brown the meat or bird, to seal, before pot-roasting.

BARBECUING MEAT, POULTRY AND GAME

Food poisoning from undercooked or overcooked meat and poultry is a barbecue risk. These rules ensure risk-free barbecuing:

• Keep all marinated meat, poultry and game in the refrigerator until ready to cook.

• Leave enough time for a charcoal barbecue to reach the right heat – about 45 minutes – before cooking. Wait until the coals are glowing red with a powdery grey surface. A gas barbecue needs ten minutes to heat.

• Do not cook over flames.

• Cook evenly over a steady heat – raising or lowering the grill above the coals as needed.

• Cook for a longer time if the temperature is lower.

• Chicken or joints of meat on the bone take longer to cook, so de-bone where possible.

• Meat, poultry and game must be piping hot in the centre with no red or pink remaining, and clear juices.

• Do not overcook – burnt meat can produce harmful chemicals.

• Turn the food regularly to avoid charring or uneven cooking.

• Never partially cook meat or poultry to reheat on a barbecue.

• Never reuse raw meat marinades.

• Keep your barbecue clean.

HOW TO CHECK IF YOUR MEAT/BIRD IS COOKED

It is important to cook meat, poultry and game properly to make sure that any harmful bacteria have been killed. The following foods should always be cooked until the juices run clear and there is no hint of red or pink remaining:

POULTRY
PHEASANT
PARTRIDGE
PORK
BURGERS
SAUSAGES
KEBABS
ROLLED JOINTS

This rule does not apply to whole cuts of meat (except pork) or joints, which can be cooked rare as long as they have been sealed properly. Steak and cutlets can also be cooked rare. Bacteria are to be found on the surface of meat, so sealing the meat in a hot frying pan or saucepan will kill any harmful bacteria. Fresh meat mince or mince products should be thoroughly cooked through to avoid any risk of food poisoning.

To check if meat, poultry or game is cooked through, insert a skewer into the thickest part of the meat. If

the juices run clear, it is cooked, but if there is any pinkness or blood, continue cooking for a few minutes and test again.

A meat thermometer is a useful device for checking if a large joint is cooked. It will register the internal

temperature of a piece of meat and provide a scale to show when the meat will be cooked. Insert the thermometer into the thickest part of the meat, making sure that it is not touching bone or fat but is well embedded in the flesh.

CARVING POULTRY AND GAME BIRDS

Smaller game birds are often served whole or halved. The same basic technique for carving applies to chicken and most other birds as follows:

- Remove the legs.
- Remove the wings.
- Carve the meat from the breast, slicing downwards, with the knife running parallel to the bird.

- Remove any remaining meat from the carcass, including the oysters – the nuggets of flesh either side of the bird on the underside – by hand. The technique of carving the breast

meat can vary to accommodate the size and shape of the bird, as follows:

Duck: Remove the legs and wings and slice the meat from the neck end. Slice close to the breastbone and loosen the breast meat before carving the first slice. Holding the knife at a 45-degree angle, cut the remaining breast meat parallel to the first slice.

Goose: Remove the legs and wings and slice the meat from the neck end. Carve long, thick slices of meat along the length of the breast, holding the knife almost flat against the meat.

Turkey: Remove the wings and legs. Carve the dark meat from the legs, holding the knuckle end of the leg and cutting downwards. Carve the breast into thin slices downwards from the fattest part of the breast on either side of the breastbone.

NUTRITION

Meat plays an important role in a balanced, healthy diet. Its key nutrients are particularly important for certain groups of people, namely the under-fives, teenagers, women of childbearing age and the elderly.

Meat is a good source of protein, and provides many vitamins and minerals such as iron, selenium, zinc and B vitamins, including the important vitamin B12, which is not present in plant foods, and vitamin D, essential for good health. A major source of easily absorbed iron, meat, eaten with vegetables and cereals, will also aid absorption of the useful amounts of iron that other foods have to offer.

Protein is essential for growth and repair of the body, so should constitute 15 per cent of our daily calorie intake. Poultry and game birds are lean and therefore an excellent source of high-protein, low-fat meat.

When buying meat, the cut you choose can vary greatly in its fat content. For instance, a lean pork leg joint for roasting has a quarter less fat than pork belly. However, fat is important for giving flavour to the meat and is also crucial to its tenderness, so if you want to remove all the visible fat, leave it in place until the meat has been cooked and then trim if necessary. So-called 'cheap' cuts of meat can often be the tastiest and most nutritious, so try experimenting with new cuts and methods of cooking.

RECOMMENDED AMOUNTS OF PROTEIN

MEN	44–55 g per day
WOMEN	42–45 g per day
CHILDREN AGED 4–6	15–20 g per day
CHILDREN AGED 7–10	23–28 g per day

2

PÂTÉS, TERRINES AND SOUPS

Try these tempting treats for melt-in-the mouth nibbles or first courses. You can create all kinds of pâtés and terrines in a matter of minutes if you've got a food processor – use these recipes to inspire you, and try variations according to your tastes. There is also a selection of hearty soups, from Chicken, Squash and Spinach Soup to Middle Eastern Soup with Harissa, which are substantial enough to serve as meals on their own.

PORK AND PISTACHIO TERRINE

Put the pork, veal, pig's liver, pork fat, brandy, garlic, parsley, salt, thyme, allspice and pepper to taste in a large bowl and use your hands to mix together. Cover and chill for at least 8–24 hours.

Preheat the oven to 160°C/325°F/ Gas Mark 3. Lightly grease the base and sides of a 1.5-litre/2³/₄-pint rectangular ceramic terrine. Put the bacon rashers on a chopping board and use the back of a knife to gently stretch until almost double in length. Use to line the base and sides of the terrine, laying them next to each other, so that the excess hangs over both long sides.

To check if the seasoning of the meat mixture needs adjusting, heat a small frying pan over a medium– high heat, add a small amount of the mixture and cook through. Taste and adjust the seasoning, if necessary. Stir the pistachio nuts into the meat mixture.

Spoon one-third of the meat mixture into the terrine, pressing it down well. Lay half the chicken slices on top, pointing from short end to short end, and add a few chives, pointing in the same direction. Repeat this layering, ending with a layer of meat mixture.

Fold over the overhanging strips of bacon to cover the top of the meat mixture. Cover the terrine with the lid and put in a roasting tin. Bring a kettle of water to the boil and pour enough water into the roasting tin to come halfway up the sides of the terrine.

Cook in the preheated oven for 1¹/₂ hours, or until the mixture pulls away from the sides of the terrine and the juices run clear. When a metal skewer is inserted into the small hole in the terrine lid, it should come out hot.

Remove the terrine from the water and leave it to stand for 5 minutes. Uncover the terrine and pour off most of the excess juices, then set aside to cool completely.

Meanwhile, position a loaf tin on top and weigh it down. Chill for 24–48 hours.

To serve, run a round-bladed knife around the edge of the terrine to loosen, then set the base in a sink of very hot water for 20–30 seconds. Put a serving dish on top of the terrine, then carefully invert both, giving a sharp shake halfway over, and lift off the terrine. Leave to return to room temperature, then use a serrated knife to slice.

MAKES 15–20 SLICES

350 g/12 oz coarsely minced fresh pork

250 g/9 oz coarsely minced fresh veal

200 g/7 oz pig's liver, finely chopped

200 g/7 oz pork fat, diced

125 ml/4 fl oz brandy

2 large garlic cloves, very finely chopped

2 tbsp chopped fresh flat-leaf parsley

1 tsp salt

³/₄ tsp dried thyme

large pinch of ground allspice

butter, for greasing

10–12 rindless unsmoked streaky bacon rashers

55 g/2 oz shelled pistachio nuts, roughly chopped

2 skinless, boneless chicken breasts, about 175 g/6 oz each, cut into thin strips

small handful of fresh chives, snipped

pepper

CHICKEN AND ASPARAGUS TIMBALES

SERVES 4

1 lemon

2 skinless, boneless chicken
breasts, about 115 g/4 oz each

2 fresh tarragon sprigs

150 ml/5 fl oz water

115 g/4 oz fresh young
asparagus spears, trimmed

2 tbsp dry white wine

10 g/¹/₄ oz powdered gelatine

100 g/3¹/₂ oz fromage frais

1 tsp chopped fresh tarragon

salt and pepper

Pare a strip of rind from the lemon. Squeeze the juice and reserve. Put the lemon rind, chicken, tarragon sprigs and water in a saucepan and season to taste with salt and pepper. Cover, bring to the boil, then reduce the heat to low and cook for 20 minutes, or until the meat is tender. Remove the chicken with a slotted spoon and leave to cool. Sieve and reserve the cooking liquid.

Bring a large saucepan of water to the boil. Add the asparagus and blanch for 5 minutes. Drain, then cut off and reserve 4 cm/1¹/₂ inches of the tips. Chop the stalks.

Put the reserved cooking liquid in a jug. Make up to 150 ml/5 fl oz with water, if necessary. Stir in the wine. Put 4 tablespoons of the mixture in a heatproof bowl, sprinkle ¹/₂ teaspoon of the gelatine on top and leave to soak for 2 minutes. Set over a saucepan of simmering water and stir for 2–3 minutes. Divide between 4 ramekins and chill for 5 minutes. Arrange 2 asparagus tips, facing in opposite directions, in each ramekin and chill until set. Dissolve the remaining gelatine in the remaining stock and wine in the same way as before.

Chop the chicken, then process in a food processor until smooth. Add the reserved lemon juice, fromage frais and gelatine mixture and mix briefly. Transfer to a bowl, stir in the asparagus stalks and chopped tarragon and season to taste with salt and pepper. Divide between the ramekins and chill for 1 hour, or until set.

To serve, dip the ramekin bases in hot water and invert onto 4 plates.

CHICKEN AND MIXED HERB PÂTÉ

Cook the diced potato in a saucepan of boiling water for 10 minutes, or until tender, then drain well.

Transfer the potato to a food processor, then add the chicken, garlic, parsley, coriander, lemon rind and juice and salt and pepper to taste. Process until thoroughly blended. Alternatively, finely chop all the ingredients and mix together until thoroughly blended.

Put the mixture in a large bowl and stir in the cream cheese. Cover and chill for 45 minutes.

Remove the pâté from the refrigerator and divide between individual serving dishes. Sprinkle over the sliced spring onion to garnish and serve with pitta bread triangles, vegetable crudités and lemon wedges.

SERVES 4

1 small floury potato, diced

250 g/9 oz cooked skinless chicken, diced

1 garlic clove, crushed

1 tbsp chopped fresh parsley

1 tbsp chopped fresh coriander

$^{1}/_{2}$ tbsp grated lemon rind

2 tbsp lemon juice

100 g/3$^{1}/_{2}$ oz cream cheese

salt and pepper

sliced spring onion, to garnish

TO SERVE

pitta bread, cut into triangles

vegetable crudités, such as carrots and celery

lemon wedges

HAM AND PARSLEY TERRINE

MAKES 15–20 SLICES

4 gelatine leaves

350 ml/12 fl oz dry white wine

250 ml/9 fl oz warm water

25 g/1 oz unsalted butter

2 shallots, very finely chopped

1 garlic clove, crushed

40 g/1^{1}/$_{2}$ oz fresh flat-leaf parsley, finely chopped

1 piece ham, weighing 300 g/10^{1}/$_{2}$ oz, cut into 1-cm/^{1}/$_{2}$-inch cubes

pepper

Put the gelatine leaves in a bowl with enough cold water to cover and leave to soak for 5 minutes. Meanwhile, put the wine and water in a saucepan over a medium heat and heat just until small bubbles begin to appear around the edge, without boiling.

Melt the butter in a saucepan over a medium heat. Add the shallots and garlic and cook, stirring frequently, for 3 minutes, or until softened but not browned. Transfer to a heatproof bowl and set aside. Stir the parsley into the bowl and add pepper to taste.

Use your hands to lift the gelatine leaves out of the water and squeeze to remove the excess liquid. Remove the saucepan with the simmering liquid from the heat, add the gelatine and stir until dissolved. Add to the parsley mixture.

Rinse the inside of a 1.5-litre/ 2^{3}/$_{4}$-pint rectangular terrine with water, but do not dry. Pour a 5-mm/^{1}/$_{4}$-inch layer of the gelatine mixture into the base of the terrine. Chill for 30 minutes, or until beginning to set.

Scatter one-third of the ham over the gelatine, pressing it slightly into the gelatine. Chill for 30 minutes, or until completely set.

Top the ham with one-third of the remaining gelatine, then chill until starting to set. Add another third of the ham and chill for 30 minutes, or until set. Continue layering and chilling until all the ingredients are used up, ending with a layer of gelatine. Cover the terrine and leave to chill at least overnight, or for up to 2 days.

To serve, run a round-bladed knife around the edge of the terrine. Put a serving dish on top of the terrine, then carefully invert both, giving a sharp shake halfway over, and lift off the terrine. Cut the terrine into slices and serve.

CHICKEN LIVER PÂTÉ

Transfer the chicken liver mixture to a food processor and process until smooth. Add the remaining butter, cut into small pieces, and process again until creamy.

Press the pâté into a serving dish or 4 small ramekins, smooth the surface and cover. Store in the refrigerator. If it is to be kept for more than 2 days, you could seal the surface by pouring over a little clarified butter and leaving to set.

Serve the pâté accompanied by brown toast fingers.

SERVES 4

140 g/5 oz butter

1 onion, finely chopped

1 garlic clove, finely chopped

250 g/9 oz chicken livers

$^{1}/_{2}$ tsp Dijon mustard

2 tbsp brandy (optional)

salt and pepper

brown toast fingers, to serve

Melt half the butter in a large frying pan over a medium heat. Add the onion and cook, stirring frequently, for 3–4 minutes until softened but not browned. Add the garlic and cook, stirring, for 2 minutes.

Check the chicken livers and remove the cores and any discoloured parts using a pair of scissors. Add the livers to the frying pan and cook over a medium–high heat, stirring frequently, for 5–6 minutes until browned all over.

Season well with salt and pepper and stir in the mustard and brandy, if using.

CONSOMMÉ WITH EGG AND LEMON SAUCE

SERVES 4–6

1.4 litres/2¹⁄₂ pints chicken stock

55 g/2 oz arborio or other short-grain rice

2 eggs

6 tbsp fresh lemon juice

salt and pepper

slices of lemon, to garnish

Pour the stock into a large saucepan and bring to the boil. Add the rice and return to the boil, then reduce the heat and simmer for 15–20 minutes, or according to the packet instructions, until tender.

Meanwhile, put the eggs and lemon juice in a bowl and whisk together until frothy.

When the rice is cooked, reduce the heat and, whisking constantly, gradually add a ladleful of the stock to the lemon mixture. Pour the mixture into the soup and simmer, still whisking, until the soup thickens slightly. (Do not boil the mixture or it will curdle.) Season to taste with salt and pepper.

Ladle the soup into individual serving bowls and garnish each with slices of lemon. Serve hot.

FRAGRANT CHICKEN SOUP

Remove the tough outer leaves from the lemon grass stalks. Using a sharp knife, slice the soft, inner parts diagonally into chunks.

Pour the coconut milk into a large, heavy-based saucepan and add the lemon grass, lime leaves and galangal. Bring to the boil, then reduce the heat and simmer for 2 minutes.

Add the water and return to the boil. Add the chicken strips, mushrooms and tomatoes, reduce the heat and simmer for 5 minutes, or until the chicken strips are cooked through and tender.

Stir in the chillies, lime juice and fish sauce. Using a slotted spoon, remove and discard the lemon grass and galangal.

Ladle into 4 large, warmed soup bowls, garnish with a few coriander leaves and serve immediately.

SERVES 4

2 lemon grass stalks

400 ml/14 fl oz coconut milk

3 kaffir lime leaves, torn into small pieces

5-cm/2-inch piece galangal or fresh root ginger, sliced

700 ml/1¼ pints water

500 g/1 lb 2 oz skinless, boneless chicken breasts, trimmed of all visible fat and cut into thin strips

225 g/8 oz shiitake mushrooms, chopped

2 tomatoes, cut into wedges

3 fresh bird's eye chillies, deseeded and thinly sliced

3 tbsp lime juice

2 tbsp Thai fish sauce

fresh coriander leaves, to garnish

BE CAREFUL WHEN HANDLING FRESH CHILLIES, AS THEY CAN BURN. WEARING RUBBER GLOVES IS A WISE PRECAUTION AND YOU SHOULD ALWAYS WASH YOUR HANDS THOROUGHLY AFTERWARDS.

CHICKEN AND PASTA SOUP WITH GUINEA FOWL

Put the chicken and guinea fowl in a large saucepan with the stock. Bring to the boil and add the onion, peppercorns, cloves and mace. Reduce the heat and simmer gently for 2 hours, or until the stock is reduced by one third.

Sieve the soup and skim off any fat. Return the soup and meat to a clean saucepan. Add the cream and slowly bring to the boil.

To make a roux, melt the butter in a small saucepan over a low heat. Add the flour and cook, stirring constantly, until it forms a paste-like consistency. Add the roux to the soup and cook, stirring constantly, until slightly thickened.

Just before serving, stir in the cooked spaghetti.

Ladle the soup into individual warmed serving bowls, garnish with the chopped parsley and serve.

SERVES 6

500 g/1 lb 2 oz skinless, boneless chicken, chopped

500 g/1 lb 2 oz skinless, boneless guinea fowl

600 ml/1 pint chicken stock

1 small onion

6 peppercorns

1 tsp cloves

pinch of mace

150 ml/5 fl oz double cream

15 g/^{1}/$_2$ oz butter

2 tsp plain flour

125 g/4^1/$_2$ oz dried spaghetti, broken into short lengths and cooked

2 tbsp chopped fresh parsley, to garnish

CHICKEN, SQUASH AND SPINACH SOUP

SERVES 4

1 tbsp butter

1 tbsp oil

3 skinless, boneless chicken breasts, about 115 g/4 oz each, cubed

2 small leeks, green parts included, thinly sliced

1 small butternut squash, peeled and cut into 2-cm/ $^3/_4$-inch cubes

1 small fresh green chilli (optional), deseeded and very finely chopped

400 g/14 oz canned chickpeas, drained and rinsed

$^1/_4$ tsp ground cumin

1 litre/1$^3/_4$ pints chicken stock

115 g/4 oz baby spinach leaves, roughly chopped

salt and pepper

warm crusty bread, to serve

Melt the butter with the oil in a large saucepan over a medium–low heat. Add the chicken, leeks, squash and chilli, if using. Cover and cook, stirring occasionally, for 10 minutes, until the vegetables are beginning to soften.

Add the chickpeas, cumin and salt and pepper to taste.

Pour in the stock. Bring to the boil, then reduce the heat and simmer gently for 40 minutes, or until the squash is tender.

Stir in the spinach and cook for a further 30 seconds, or until the spinach is just wilted.

Serve the soup immediately with warm, crusty bread.

DUCK WITH SPRING ONION SOUP

SERVES 4

2 duck breasts, about 175 g/
6 oz each, skin on

2 tbsp Thai red curry paste

2 tbsp vegetable or
groundnut oil

bunch of spring onions,
chopped

2 garlic cloves, crushed

5-cm/2-inch piece fresh root
ginger, grated

2 carrots, thinly sliced

1 red pepper, deseeded and cut
into strips

1 litre/1¾ pints chicken stock

2 tbsp sweet chilli sauce

3–4 tbsp Thai soy sauce

400 g/14 oz canned straw
mushrooms, drained

Slash the skin of the duck 3 or 4 times with a sharp knife and rub in the curry paste.

Heat a wok or large frying pan over a high heat. Add the duck breasts, skin-side down, and cook for 2–3 minutes. Turn over, reduce the heat and cook for a further 3–4 minutes, or until tender and the juices run clear when a skewer is inserted into the thickest part of the meat. Remove with a slotted spoon and thickly slice. Keep warm.

Heat the oil in the preheated wok or large frying pan over a high heat. Add half the spring onions, the garlic, ginger, carrots and red pepper and stir-fry for 2–3 minutes. Pour in the stock and add the chilli sauce, soy sauce and mushrooms. Bring to the boil, then reduce the heat and simmer for 4–5 minutes.

Ladle the soup into warmed bowls, top with the duck slices and garnish with the remaining spring onions. Serve immediately.

SPICY BEEF AND NOODLE SOUP

Pour the stock into a large saucepan and bring to the boil. Meanwhile, heat the oil in a preheated wok or large frying pan over a high heat. Add one third of the noodles and cook, stirring, for 10–20 seconds, or until puffed up. Lift out with tongs, drain on kitchen paper and set aside. Pour off all but 2 tablespoons of the oil.

Add the shallots, garlic and ginger to the wok and stir-fry for 1 minute. Add the beef and curry paste and stir-fry for 3–4 minutes until tender.

Transfer the beef mixture to the stock with the uncooked noodles, soy sauce and fish sauce. Simmer for 2–3 minutes until the noodles have swelled.

Serve the soup hot, garnished with chopped coriander and the reserved crispy noodles.

SERVES 4

1 litre/1³/₄ pints beef stock

150 ml/5 fl oz vegetable or groundnut oil

85 g/3 oz dried rice vermicelli noodles

2 shallots, thinly sliced

2 garlic cloves, crushed

2.5-cm/1-inch piece fresh root ginger, thinly sliced

1 fillet steak, weighing 225 g/ 8 oz, cut into thin strips

2 tbsp Thai green curry paste

2 tbsp Thai soy sauce

1 tbsp Thai fish sauce

chopped fresh coriander, to garnish

MINCED BEEF AND BEAN SOUP

SERVES 4

2 tbsp vegetable oil

1 large onion, finely chopped

2 garlic cloves, finely chopped

1 green pepper, deseeded
and sliced

2 carrots, sliced

400 g/14 oz canned
black-eyed beans

225 g/8 oz fresh beef mince

1 tsp each ground cumin, chilli
powder and paprika

¼ cabbage, sliced

225 g/8 oz tomatoes, peeled
and chopped

600 ml/1 pint beef stock

salt and pepper

tortilla chips, warmed corn
tortillas or flour tortillas,
to serve

Heat the oil in a large saucepan over a medium heat. Add the onion and garlic and cook, stirring frequently, for 5 minutes, or until softened. Add the green pepper and carrots and cook, stirring frequently, for 5 minutes.

Meanwhile, drain the beans, reserving the liquid from the can. Put two-thirds of the beans, reserving the remainder, in a food processor or blender with the bean liquid and process until smooth.

Add the mince to the saucepan and cook, stirring constantly with a wooden spoon to break up the meat, until browned all over. Add the spices and cook, stirring, for 2 minutes. Add the cabbage, tomatoes, stock and puréed beans and season to taste with salt and pepper. Bring to the boil, then reduce the heat, cover and simmer for 15 minutes, or until the vegetables are tender.

Stir in the reserved beans, cover and simmer for a further 5 minutes.

Ladle the soup into 4 warmed soup bowls and serve with a bowl of tortilla chips or some warmed corn tortillas or flour tortillas.

MINCED BEEF AND CORIANDER SOUP

SERVES 4–6

225 g/8 oz fresh beef mince

1.5 litres/2³/₄ pints
chicken stock

3 egg whites, lightly beaten

1 tsp salt

¹/₂ tsp white pepper

MARINADE

1 tsp salt

1 tsp sugar

1 tsp Shaoxing rice wine
or dry sherry

1 tsp light soy sauce

TO SERVE

1 tbsp finely chopped fresh
root ginger

1 tbsp finely chopped
spring onions

4–5 tbsp finely chopped
fresh coriander, tough stalks
discarded

Mix all the ingredients for the marinade together in a bowl. Add the mince and turn to coat in the marinade, then cover and leave to marinate in the refrigerator for 20 minutes.

Pour the stock into a large saucepan and bring to the boil. Add the marinated mince, stirring to break up any clumps, and simmer for 10 minutes.

Slowly add the egg whites, stirring rapidly so that they form fine shreds. Season to taste with salt and pepper.

To serve, divide the ginger, spring onions and coriander between the bases of individual bowls and pour the soup on top.

MIDDLE EASTERN SOUP WITH HARISSA

SERVES 6

2 aubergines

3 tbsp olive oil

6 lamb shanks

1 small onion, chopped

400 ml/14 fl oz chicken stock

2 litres/3^1/$_2$ pints water

400 g/14 oz sweet potato, cut into chunks

5-cm/2-inch piece cinnamon stick

1 tsp ground cumin

2 tbsp chopped fresh coriander

HARISSA

2 red peppers, roasted, peeled, deseeded and chopped

^{1}/$_2$ tsp coriander seeds, dry-fried

25 g/1 oz fresh red chillies, chopped

2 garlic cloves, chopped

2 tsp caraway seeds

olive oil

salt

Preheat the oven to 200°C/400°F/ Gas Mark 6. Prick the aubergines all over with a fork, put on a baking sheet and bake in the preheated oven for 1 hour. Leave to cool, then peel and chop.

Heat the oil in a saucepan over a high heat. Add the lamb shanks and cook until browned all over. Add the onion, stock and water. Bring to the boil, then reduce the heat and simmer for 1 hour.

Meanwhile, to make the harissa, put the red peppers, coriander seeds, chillies, garlic and caraway seeds in a food processor and process until well blended. With the

motor running, add enough oil through the feed tube to make a paste. Season to taste with salt, then spoon into a jar. Cover with a layer of oil, seal and chill.

Remove the lamb shanks from the stock, cut off the meat and chop. Add the sweet potato and spices to the stock and bring to the boil. Reduce the heat, cover and simmer for 20 minutes. Remove the cinnamon stick. Transfer to the food processor and process with the aubergine until smooth. Return to the saucepan, add the lamb and coriander and heat until hot. Serve with the harissa.

BACON AND LENTIL SOUP

Heat a large, heavy-based saucepan or flameproof casserole over a medium heat. Add the bacon and cook, stirring frequently, for 4–5 minutes, or until the fat runs.

Stir in the onion, carrots, celery, turnip and potato and cook, stirring frequently, for 5 minutes, or until beginning to soften.

Add the lentils and bouquet garni and pour in the water. Bring to the boil, then reduce the heat, cover and simmer for 1 hour, or until the lentils are tender.

Remove the bouquet garni and season the soup to taste with pepper, and salt if necessary.

Ladle into warmed soup bowls and serve immediately.

SERVES 4

450 g/1 lb rindless thick smoked bacon rashers, diced

1 onion, chopped

2 carrots, sliced

2 celery sticks, chopped

1 turnip, chopped

1 large potato, chopped

85 g/3 oz Puy lentils

1 bouquet garni

1 litre/1³/₄ pints water or chicken stock

salt and pepper

Do not add any salt until the lentils have finished cooking, otherwise they will toughen, which will impair the texture of the soup.

SWEETCORN, CHORIZO AND SMOKED CHILLI SOUP

SERVES 6

1 tbsp sunflower or corn oil

2 onions, chopped

550 g/1 lb 4 oz frozen sweetcorn kernels, thawed

600 ml/1 pint chicken stock

425 ml/15 fl oz milk

4 chipotle chillies, deseeded and finely chopped

2 garlic cloves, finely chopped

55 g/2 oz thinly sliced chorizo sausage, casings removed

2 tbsp lime juice

2 tbsp chopped fresh coriander

salt

Heat the oil in a large, heavy-based saucepan over a low heat. Add the onions and cook, stirring occasionally, for 5 minutes, or until softened. Stir in the sweetcorn kernels, cover and cook for a further 3 minutes.

Add the stock, half the milk, the chillies and garlic and season to taste with salt. Bring to the boil, then reduce the heat, cover and simmer for 15–20 minutes.

Stir in the remaining milk. Reserve about 175 ml/6 fl oz of the soup solids, draining off as much liquid as possible. Transfer the remaining soup solids to a food processor or blender and process to a coarse purée.

Return the soup purée to the saucepan and stir in the reserved soup solids, the chorizo, lime juice and coriander.

Reheat the soup to simmering point, stirring constantly.

Ladle the soup into warmed soup bowls and serve immediately.

3

STARTERS AND SAVOURIES

Whether you're cooking for an informal get-together or for a special occasion, these recipes are easy to prepare but impressive in effect. Choose from classic favourites, such as Devils and Angels on Horseback, Roasted Asparagus with Ham or Duck Salad, or try out new options, such as Chicken and Spinach Salad with Ginger Dressing, or Polenta with Parma Ham. There are also many substantial yet familiar savoury snacks with an international twist for you to enjoy, from Croque Monsieur and Cheesesteak Sandwiches, to Spring Rolls and Beef Teriyaki Kebabs.

CROQUE MONSIEUR

Spread half the cheese on 2 slices of bread, then top each with a slice of ham, cut to fit. Sprinkle the ham with all but 2 tablespoons of the remaining cheese, then add the top slices of bread and press down.

To make the white sauce, melt the butter with the oil in a small, heavy-based saucepan over a medium heat. Add the flour and cook, stirring constantly, for 1 minute. Remove from the heat and pour in the milk, stirring constantly. Return to the heat and cook, stirring constantly, for a minute or so until the sauce is smooth and thickened. Remove the sauce from the heat and stir in the remaining cheese and pepper to taste, then set aside and keep warm.

Beat the egg in a soup plate or other flat bowl. Add one sandwich and press down to coat on both sides, then remove from the bowl and repeat with the other sandwich.

Preheat the grill to high. Line a baking tray with foil and set aside. Melt the butter in a sauté or frying pan over a medium–high heat. Add one or both sandwiches, depending on the size of your pan, and cook until golden brown on both sides. Add a little extra butter, if necessary, if you have to cook the sandwiches separately.

Transfer the sandwiches to the foil-lined baking tray and spread the white sauce over the top. Cook under the preheated grill, about 10 cm/4 inches from the heat, for 4 minutes until golden and brown.

SERVES 2

100 g/3½ oz Gruyère or Emmenthal cheese, grated

4 slices white bread, crusts trimmed

2 thick slices cooked ham

1 small egg

40 g/1½ oz unsalted butter

WHITE SAUCE

25 g/1 oz unsalted butter

1 tsp sunflower oil

½ tbsp plain flour

125 ml/4 fl oz warm milk

pepper

WHEN CROQUE MADAME IS LISTED ON A MENU, IT MEANS A FRIED EGG WILL BE ADDED TO THE HAM AND CHEESE FILLING. FOR A MORE ROBUST FLAVOUR, SPREAD THE BREAD WITH DIJON OR WHOLEGRAIN MUSTARD BEFORE ADDING THE HAM AND CHEESE.

SERVES 4

350 g/12 oz boneless rib steak

1 French stick

3 tbsp olive oil

1 onion, thinly sliced

1 green pepper, deseeded and thinly sliced

75 g/2³/₄ oz halloumi or mozzarella cheese, thinly sliced

salt and pepper

hot pepper sauce, to serve

CHEESESTEAK SANDWICHES

Put the steak in the freezer for about 2 hours before you need it, until partially frozen.

Cut the French stick into 4 equal lengths, then cut each piece horizontally in half. Thinly slice the partially frozen steak across the grain of the meat.

Heat 2 tablespoons of the oil in a large frying pan over a medium heat. Add the onion and green pepper and cook, stirring occasionally, for 10–15 minutes until both vegetables are softened and the onion is golden brown. Push the mixture to one side of the frying pan.

Heat the remaining oil in the frying pan over a medium heat. When hot, add the steak and stir-fry for 4–5 minutes until tender. Stir the onion mixture and steak together and season to taste with salt and pepper.

Preheat the grill to medium. Divide the steak mixture between the 4 bottom halves of bread and top with the cheese. Cook under the preheated grill for 1–2 minutes until the cheese has melted, then cover with the top halves of bread and press down gently. Serve immediately with hot pepper sauce.

SPRING ROLLS

MAKES 20–25

6 dried shiitake mushrooms, soaked in warm water for 20 minutes

1 tbsp vegetable or groundnut oil, plus extra for deep-frying

225 g/8 oz fresh pork mince

1 tsp dark soy sauce

100 g/3½ oz canned bamboo shoots, rinsed, drained and cut into matchsticks, or fresh bamboo shoots, boiled in water for 30 minutes, drained and cut into matchsticks

pinch of salt

100 g/3½ oz raw prawns, peeled, deveined and chopped

225 g/8 oz fresh beansprouts, roughly chopped

1 tbsp finely chopped spring onions

25 spring roll wrappers

1 egg white, lightly beaten

Squeeze out any excess water from the mushrooms and finely slice, discarding any tough stems.

Heat the oil in a preheated wok or deep saucepan over a high heat. Add the pork and stir-fry until browned. Add the soy sauce, bamboo shoots, mushrooms and salt and stir-fry for 3 minutes.

Add the prawns and stir-fry for 2 minutes. Add the beansprouts and stir-fry for 1 minute. Remove from the heat and stir in the spring onions. Leave to cool.

Put a tablespoon of the mixture towards the bottom of a wrapper. Roll once to secure the filling, then fold in the sides to create a 10-cm/ 4-inch piece and continue to roll up. Seal with egg white.

Heat the oil for deep-frying in a wok, deep-fat fryer or large, heavy-based saucepan to 180–190°C/ 350–375°F, or until a cube of bread browns in 30 seconds. Add the rolls, in batches, and cook for 5 minutes, or until golden brown and crisp. Remove with a slotted spoon and drain on kitchen paper. Keep hot while you cook the remaining rolls.

CRISPY PORK AND PEANUT BASKETS

Preheat the oven to 200°C/400°F/ Gas Mark 6. Cut each sheet of filo pastry into 24 squares, 7 cm/ $2^3/4$ inches across, to make a total of 48 squares. Brush each square lightly with a little of the oil and arrange the squares in stacks of 4 in 12 small patty tins, pointing outwards. Press the pastry down into the patty tins.

Bake the pastry cases in the preheated oven for 6–8 minutes until golden brown.

Meanwhile, heat the remaining oil in a preheated wok over a high heat. Add the garlic and stir-fry for 30 seconds. Add the pork and stir-fry for 4–5 minutes until browned.

Add the curry paste and spring onions and stir-fry for 1 minute. Stir in the peanut butter, soy sauce and chopped coriander. Season to taste with salt and pepper.

Spoon the pork mixture into the filo baskets and serve immediately, garnished with coriander sprigs.

MAKES 12

2 sheets filo pastry, each about 42 x 28 cm/16^1/$_2$ x 11 inches

2 tbsp vegetable oil

1 garlic clove, crushed

125 g/4^1/$_2$ oz fresh pork mince

1 tsp Thai red curry paste

2 spring onions, finely chopped

3 tbsp crunchy peanut butter

1 tbsp light soy sauce

1 tbsp chopped fresh coriander, plus extra sprigs to garnish

salt and pepper

WHEN USING FILO PASTRY, REMEMBER THAT IT DRIES OUT VERY QUICKLY AND BECOMES BRITTLE AND DIFFICULT TO HANDLE. WORK QUICKLY AND KEEP ANY SHEETS OF PASTRY YOU'RE NOT USING COVERED WITH CLINGFILM AND A DAMPENED CLOTH.

DEVILS AND ANGELS ON HORSEBACK

Preheat the oven to 200°C/400°F/ Gas Mark 6.

For the devils, cut each bacon rasher lengthways in half. Put on a chopping board and use the back of a knife to stretch gently until almost double in length. Cut each anchovy fillet lengthways in half. Wrap an anchovy half around each almond and press them into the cavities in the prunes where the stones have been removed. Wrap a bacon strip around each prune and secure with a cocktail stick.

For the angels, cut each bacon rasher lengthways in half. Put on a chopping board and use the back of a knife to stretch gently until almost double in length. Wrap a bacon strip around each oyster and secure with a cocktail stick.

Put the devils and angels on a baking sheet and cook in the preheated oven for 10–15 minutes until sizzling hot and the bacon is cooked. Serve hot.

MAKES 32

DEVILS

8 rindless back bacon rashers

8 canned anchovy fillets, drained

16 blanched almonds

16 ready-to-eat prunes

ANGELS

8 rindless back bacon rashers

16 smoked oysters, drained if canned

POLENTA WITH PARMA HAM

SERVES 6

600 ml/1 pint water

70 g/2$\frac{1}{2}$ oz quick-cook polenta

25 g/1 oz freshly grated Parmesan cheese

2 tbsp butter, softened

salt and pepper

2 tbsp extra virgin olive oil, plus extra to serve

TOPPING

6 slices Parma ham

85 g/3 oz fontina cheese, cut into 6 slices

12 fresh sage leaves

extra virgin olive oil, for oiling

Line a 15 x 25-cm/6 x 10-inch Swiss roll tin with baking paper and set aside.

Pour the water into a large saucepan and bring to the boil. Reduce the heat so that it is just simmering and add a large pinch of salt. Add the polenta in a steady stream, stirring constantly. Simmer, stirring constantly, for 5 minutes, or until thickened.

Remove from the heat and stir in the Parmesan cheese and butter and season to taste with pepper. Spoon the polenta evenly into the prepared tin and smooth the surface with a palette knife. Set aside to cool completely.

Preheat the grill to high. Oil a baking sheet and a 7.5-cm/3-inch plain, round pastry cutter. Turn out the polenta onto a work surface, stamp out 6 rounds and put on the prepared baking sheet. Brush generously with some of the oil and season to taste with salt and pepper.

Cook under the preheated grill for 3–4 minutes. Turn the rounds over, brush with more of the oil and cook for a further 3–4 minutes until golden. Remove from the grill and, if you are not serving immediately, set the rounds aside to cool completely.

Drape a slice of ham on each round and top with a slice of fontina cheese. Brush the sage leaves with the remaining oil and put 2 on each round.

Cook the polenta rounds under the preheated grill for 3–4 minutes until the cheese has melted and the sage is crisp. Serve immediately, with extra oil for dipping.

CHICKEN GOUJONS

Put the chicken breasts between 2 sheets of clingfilm and beat with the flat end of a meat mallet or with the side of a rolling pin until about 5 mm/$\frac{1}{4}$ inch thick. Slice the chicken diagonally into 2.5-cm/1-inch strips. Put the flour in a polythene bag, add the chicken strips, a few at a time, and shake well to coat each piece.

Heat the oil for deep-frying in a large, heavy-based saucepan to 180–190°C/350–375°F, or until a cube of bread browns in 30 seconds. Meanwhile, mix together the breadcrumbs, coriander, paprika and salt and pepper to taste and spread out on a plate. Beat the eggs in a soup plate or other flat bowl. Dip the chicken strips in the egg and then in the breadcrumb mixture. When the oil is hot, add the goujons, in batches, and cook until crisp and golden all over. Remove with a slotted spoon and drain on kitchen paper. Keep hot while you cook the remaining goujons.

Meanwhile, to make the dip, mix the cream cheese, soured cream and chives together in a serving bowl, season to taste with salt and pepper and sprinkle with paprika. Transfer the goujons to a large serving plate and garnish with lemon wedges. Garnish the dip with chives and serve with the goujons.

SERVES 4

4 skinless, boneless chicken breasts, about 115 g/4 oz each

3 tbsp plain flour

sunflower oil, for deep-frying

175 g/6 oz dried breadcrumbs

1 tsp ground coriander

2 tsp paprika

2 eggs

salt and pepper

CHEESE AND CHIVE DIP

115 g/4 oz cream cheese

150 ml/5 fl oz soured cream

3 tbsp snipped fresh chives, plus extra whole chives to garnish

paprika, for sprinkling

salt and pepper

lemon wedges, to garnish

WHEN DEEP-FRYING, MAKE SURE THAT THE OIL IS AT THE CORRECT TEMPERATURE BEFORE COOKING. IF IT IS TOO HOT, IT WILL BURN THE FOOD ON THE OUTSIDE, BUT LEAVE THE INSIDE RAW.

CREAMY CHICKEN RAVIOLI

To make the Pasta Dough, sift the flour and a pinch of salt onto a clean work surface, make a well in the centre and pour in the eggs and oil. Using your fingers, gradually combine the eggs and oil and incorporate the flour. Turn out the dough onto a lightly floured work surface and knead until smooth. Halve the dough, wrap each half in clingfilm and leave to rest for 30 minutes before using.

Place the chicken, spinach, Parma ham and shallot in a food processor and process until blended. Transfer to a bowl, stir in 2 tablespoons of the cheese, the nutmeg and half the egg. Season with salt and pepper.

Thinly roll out half the Pasta Dough on a lightly floured work surface. Cover with a tea towel and roll out the second piece of dough. Place small mounds of the filling in rows 4 cm/1½ inches apart on one sheet of dough and brush the spaces in between with beaten egg. Place the second piece of dough on top. Press down firmly between the mounds, pushing out any air. Cut into squares, place on a floured tea towel and leave to rest for 1 hour.

Bring a large saucepan of lightly salted water to the boil. Add the ravioli in batches, return to the boil and cook for 5 minutes. Remove with a slotted spoon and drain on kitchen paper, then transfer to a warmed dish.

Meanwhile, pour the cream into a frying pan, add the garlic and bring to the boil. Simmer for 1 minute, then add the mushrooms and 2 tablespoons of the remaining cheese. Season to taste and simmer for 3 minutes. Stir in the basil, then pour the sauce over the ravioli. Sprinkle with the remaining cheese, garnish with basil sprigs and serve.

SERVES 4

115 g/4 oz cooked skinless, boneless chicken breast, roughly chopped

55 g/2 oz cooked spinach leaves

55 g/2 oz Parma ham, roughly chopped

1 shallot, roughly chopped

6 tbsp freshly grated pecorino cheese

pinch of freshly grated nutmeg

2 eggs, lightly beaten

plain white flour, for dusting

300 ml/10 fl oz double cream

2 garlic cloves, finely chopped

115 g/4 oz chestnut mushrooms thinly sliced

2 tbsp shredded fresh basil

salt and pepper

fresh basil sprigs, to garnish

PASTA DOUGH

200 g/7 oz plain white flour, plus extra for dusting

2 eggs, lightly beaten

1 tbsp olive oil

TO COOK THE CHICKEN BREAST, PUT IT IN A SAUCEPAN WITH 1 TABLESPOON LEMON JUICE AND JUST ENOUGH WATER TO COVER. SEASON TO TASTE WITH SALT AND PEPPER AND POACH GENTLY FOR 10 MINUTES, OR UNTIL COOKED.

CORONATION CHICKEN

Put the chicken breasts in a large saucepan with the bay leaf, onion and carrot. Cover with water and add ¹/₂ teaspoon salt and the peppercorns. Bring to the boil over a medium heat, then reduce the heat and simmer very gently for 20–25 minutes. Remove from the heat and leave the chicken to cool in the stock. Reserve 150 ml/5 fl oz of the stock for the sauce.

Meanwhile, heat the oil in a frying pan over a low heat. Add the shallots and cook, stirring, for 2–3 minutes until softened but not browned. Stir in the curry paste and cook for a further 1 minute. Stir in the reserved stock, the tomato purée and the lemon juice and simmer for 10 minutes until the sauce is quite thick. Leave to cool. Remove the chicken from the stock, remove and discard the skin and slice the meat into neat pieces.

Mix the mayonnaise and yogurt together and stir into the sauce. Add the apricots and season to taste with salt and pepper.

Add the chicken to the sauce and stir until well coated. Turn into a serving dish. Cover and chill for at least 1 hour to allow the flavours to mingle. Serve garnished with the chopped parsley.

SERVES 6

4 skinless, boneless chicken breasts, about 115 g/4 oz each

1 bay leaf

1 small onion, sliced

1 carrot, sliced

4 black peppercorns

1 tbsp olive oil

2 shallots, finely chopped

2 tsp mild curry paste

2 tsp tomato purée

juice of ¹/₂ lemon

300 ml/10 fl oz mayonnaise

150 ml/5 fl oz natural yogurt

85 g/3 oz ready-to-eat dried apricots, chopped

salt and pepper

2 tbsp chopped fresh parsley, to garnish

BEEF TERIYAKI KEBABS

Put the steaks in a shallow, non-metallic dish. To make the sauce, mix the cornflour and rice wine together in a small bowl, then stir in the remaining sauce ingredients. Pour the sauce over the meat, cover and leave to marinate in the refrigerator for at least 2 hours.

Preheat the barbecue. Remove the meat from the sauce and reserve. Pour the sauce into a small saucepan and bring to the boil. Reduce the heat until it is just simmering, stirring occasionally.

Cut the meat into thin strips and thread, concertina-style, onto several presoaked wooden skewers, alternating each strip of meat with the pieces of yellow pepper and spring onion. Cook the kebabs over hot coals for 5–8 minutes, or until the steak is cooked through, turning frequently and basting with the sauce once, halfway through the cooking time.

Arrange the skewers on serving plates and pour over the remaining sauce. Serve with salad leaves.

SERVES 4

450 g/1 lb extra-thin beef steaks

1 yellow pepper, deseeded and cut into chunks

8 spring onions, cut into short lengths

salad leaves, to serve

SAUCE

1 tsp cornflour

2 tbsp Shaoxing rice wine or dry sherry

2 tbsp white wine vinegar

3 tbsp soy sauce

1 tbsp dark muscovado sugar

1 garlic clove, crushed

$1/2$ tsp ground cinnamon

$1/2$ tsp ground ginger

ROASTED ASPARAGUS
WITH HAM

To make the Romesco Sauce, preheat the oven to 180°C/350°F/Gas Mark 4. Place the tomatoes, almonds and garlic on a baking sheet and roast in the preheated oven for 20 minutes, but check the almonds after about 7 minutes, because they can burn quickly; remove as soon as they are golden and giving off an aroma.

Peel the roasted garlic and tomatoes. Put the almonds, garlic,

sweet chilli and dried red chillies in a food processor and process until finely chopped. Add the tomatoes and sugar and process again.

With the motor running, slowly add the olive oil through the feed tube. Add 1½ tablespoons of the vinegar and quickly process. Taste and add extra vinegar, if desired, and salt and pepper to taste. Leave to stand for at least 2 hours.

Meanwhile, increase the oven temperature to 220°C/425°F/Gas Mark 7. Sprinkle a layer of sea salt over the base of a roasting tin that will hold the asparagus spears in a single layer. Brush the asparagus with the oil, then lay the spears in the roasting tin.

Roast in the preheated oven for 12–15 minutes until just tender when pierced with the tip of a knife. Remove from the oven and season to taste with pepper.

As soon as the spears are cool enough to handle, wrap a piece of ham around each.

Arrange on a serving platter and serve hot, warm or at room temperature with a small bowl of Romesco Sauce for dipping. Alternatively, serve on individual plates with a little Romesco Sauce.

SERVES 4–6

24 fresh young asparagus spears, trimmed

1–2 tbsp extra virgin olive oil

12 thin slices serrano ham, halved lengthways

sea salt and pepper

ROMESCO SAUCE

4 large, ripe tomatoes

16 blanched almonds

3 large garlic cloves, unpeeled and left whole

1 dried sweet chilli, soaked for 20 minutes and patted dry

4 dried red chillies, soaked for 20 minutes and patted dry

pinch of sugar

150 ml/5 fl oz extra virgin olive oil

about 2 tbsp red wine vinegar

salt and pepper

TURKEY AND RICE SALAD

SERVES 4

1 litre/1³/₄ pints chicken stock

175 g/6 oz mixed long-grain and wild rice

2 tbsp sunflower or corn oil

225 g/8 oz skinless, boneless turkey breast, trimmed of all visible fat and cut into thin strips

225 g/8 oz mangetout

115 g/4 oz oyster mushrooms, torn into pieces

55 g/2 oz shelled pistachio nuts, finely chopped

2 tbsp chopped fresh coriander

1 tbsp snipped fresh garlic chives, plus extra whole garlic chives to garnish

1 tbsp balsamic vinegar

salt and pepper

Reserve 3 tablespoons of the stock and pour the remainder into a large saucepan and bring to the boil. Add the rice and cook for 30 minutes, or until tender. Drain and leave to cool slightly.

Meanwhile, heat 1 tablespoon of the oil in a preheated wok or large frying pan over a medium heat. Add the turkey and stir-fry for 3–4 minutes, or until cooked through. Using a slotted spoon, transfer the turkey to a dish. Add the mangetout and mushrooms to the wok and stir-fry for 1 minute. Add the reserved stock and bring to the boil, then reduce the heat, cover and simmer for 3–4 minutes. Transfer the vegetables to the dish and leave to cool slightly.

Thoroughly mix the rice, turkey, mangetout, mushrooms, pistachio nuts, coriander and snipped garlic chives together, then season to taste with salt and pepper. Drizzle with the remaining oil and the vinegar and garnish with whole garlic chives. Serve warm.

BEFORE ADDING ANY OF THE INGREDIENTS TO THE PREHEATED WOK, SWIRL THE OIL GENTLY AND CAREFULLY SO THAT IT COATS THE SIDE AS WELL AS THE BASE OF THE WOK.

CHICKEN AND SPINACH SALAD WITH GINGER DRESSING

SERVES 4

250 g/9 oz baby spinach leaves

3 celery sticks, thinly sliced

$^1/_2$ cucumber

2 spring onions

3 tbsp chopped fresh parsley

350 g/12 oz boneless roast chicken, thinly sliced

smoked almonds, to garnish (optional)

DRESSING

2.5-cm/1-inch piece fresh root ginger, finely grated

3 tbsp olive oil

1 tbsp white wine vinegar

1 tbsp clear honey

$^1/_2$ tsp ground cinnamon

salt and pepper, to taste

Thoroughly wash the spinach leaves, then pat dry with kitchen paper.

Using a sharp knife, thinly slice the celery, cucumber and spring onions. Toss in a large bowl with the spinach leaves and parsley.

Transfer to serving plates and arrange the chicken on top of the salad.

Put all the ingredients for the dressing into a screw-top jar, screw the lid on tightly and shake well to mix. Pour over the salad.

Garnish the salad with a few smoked almonds, if you like, and serve immediately.

MIXED LEAVES WITH WARM CHICKEN LIVERS

Toss the salad leaves with the parsley and chives and divide between individual plates.

Heat 2 tablespoons of the oil in a sauté or frying pan over a medium–high heat. Add the shallots and garlic and cook, stirring, for 2 minutes, or until the shallots are softened but not browned.

Add another tablespoon of the oil to the pan and heat. Add the chicken livers and cook, stirring frequently, for 5 minutes, or until just pink in the centre when you cut a piece in half. Add a little extra oil to the pan while the chicken livers are cooking, if necessary.

Increase the heat to high, add the vinegar and quickly stir around. Season to taste with salt and pepper, then spoon the chicken livers and their cooking juices over the mixed leaves. Serve immediately with French bread.

SERVES 6–8

250 g/9 oz mixed salad leaves, large ones torn into bite-sized pieces

2 tbsp chopped fresh flat-leaf parsley

2 tbsp snipped fresh chives

3–4 tbsp olive oil

100 g/3^1/$_2$ oz shallots, finely chopped

1 large garlic clove, finely chopped

500 g/1 lb 2 oz chicken livers, cored, trimmed and halved

3 tbsp raspberry vinegar

salt and pepper

French bread, to serve

TO REPLICATE AN AUTHENTIC FRENCH BISTRO FLAVOUR, BUY A BAG OF MIXED LEAVES THAT INCLUDES LAMB'S LETTUCE AND ROCKET. FRESH CRESS, ESCAROLE, CURLY ENDIVE, OAK-LEAF LETTUCE AND YOUNG SPINACH LEAVES ARE ALSO IDEAL SALAD LEAVES TO INCLUDE.

DUCK SALAD

SERVES 4

4 boneless duck breasts, about 175 g/6 oz each, skin on

1 lemon grass stalk, broken into 3 and each piece cut in half lengthways

3 tbsp vegetable or groundnut oil

2 tbsp sesame oil

1 tsp Thai fish sauce

1 fresh green chilli, deseeded and chopped

2 tbsp Thai red curry paste

$^{1}/_{2}$ fresh pineapple, peeled and sliced

7.5-cm/3-inch piece cucumber, peeled, deseeded and sliced

3 tomatoes, cut into wedges

1 onion, thinly sliced

DRESSING

juice of 1 lemon

2 garlic cloves, crushed

1 tsp palm sugar or soft light brown sugar

2 tbsp vegetable or groundnut oil

Unwrap the duck breasts and leave the skin to dry out overnight in the refrigerator.

The following day, slash the skin side 5 or 6 times with a sharp knife. Mix the lemon grass, 2 tablespoons of the vegetable oil, the sesame oil, fish sauce, chilli and curry paste together in a shallow dish and add the duck breasts. Turn to coat in the marinade and rub into the meat. Cover and leave to marinate in the refrigerator for 2–3 hours.

Heat the remaining oil in a preheated wok or large frying pan over a medium heat. Add the duck, skin-side down, and cook for 3–4 minutes until the skin is browned and crisp and the meat cooked most of the way through.

Turn the breasts over and cook until browned and the meat is cooked to your liking.

Meanwhile, arrange the pineapple, cucumber, tomatoes and onion on a platter. Whisk all the ingredients for the dressing together in a small bowl and pour over the top.

Remove the duck from the wok with a slotted spoon and thickly slice. Arrange on top of the salad and serve while still hot.

STEAK WALDORF SALAD

SERVES 4

2 fillet steaks, about 175 g/6 oz each and 2.5 cm/1 inch thick

olive or sunflower oil, for brushing

1 tbsp wholegrain mustard

150 ml/5 fl oz mayonnaise

1 tbsp lemon juice

500 g/1 lb 2 oz eating apples

4 celery sticks, thinly sliced

70 g/2½ oz walnut halves, broken into pieces

100 g/3½ oz mixed salad leaves

pepper

Heat a thick, cast-iron griddle pan or heavy-based frying pan over a medium heat. Brush each steak with oil and season to taste with pepper. When hot, add the steaks to the pan and cook for 6–7 minutes for rare or 8–10 minutes for medium, turning the steaks frequently and brushing once or twice with oil. Remove from the pan and reserve.

Meanwhile, stir the mustard into the mayonnaise. Put the lemon juice into a large bowl. Peel and core the apples, then cut into small chunks and immediately toss in the lemon juice to prevent discoloration. Stir in the mustard mayonnaise. Add the celery and walnuts and toss together.

Arrange the salad leaves on 4 plates, then divide the apple mixture between them. Very thinly slice the steaks, arrange on top of the salad and serve immediately.

PEPPERED BEEF SALAD

Rinse the steaks and pat dry with kitchen paper. Mix the peppercorns with the five-spice powder and press onto both sides of the steaks.

Heat a ridged griddle pan over a high heat or preheat a grill to high. Cook the steaks in the hot pan or under the preheated grill for 2–3 minutes each side, or until cooked to your liking.

Meanwhile, mix the beansprouts, half the ginger, the shallots and red pepper together in a bowl and divide between 4 plates. Mix the remaining ginger, soy sauce, chillies, lemon grass and oils together in a separate small bowl.

Slice the beef and arrange on the vegetables. Drizzle with the dressing and serve immediately.

SERVES 4

4 fillet steaks, about 115 g/ 4 oz each

2 tbsp black peppercorns, crushed

1 tsp Chinese five-spice powder

115 g/4 oz fresh beansprouts

2.5-cm/1-inch piece fresh root ginger, finely chopped

4 shallots, thinly sliced

1 red pepper, deseeded and thinly sliced

3 tbsp Thai soy sauce

2 fresh red chillies, deseeded and sliced

$1/2$ lemon grass stalk, finely chopped

3 tbsp vegetable or groundnut oil

1 tbsp sesame oil

ARTICHOKE AND PARMA HAM SALAD

Make sure that the artichoke hearts are thoroughly drained, then cut into quarters and put in a bowl. Cut each fresh tomato into wedges. Slice the sun-dried tomatoes into thin strips. Cut the Parma ham into thin strips and add to the bowl with the tomatoes and olive halves.

Reserving a few whole basil leaves for garnishing, tear the remainder into small pieces and add to the bowl containing the other salad ingredients.

Put all the ingredients for the dressing into a screw-top jar, screw the lid on tightly and shake well to mix.

Pour the dressing over the salad and toss together. Serve the salad immediately, garnished with the reserved basil leaves.

SERVES 4

275 g/9½ oz canned artichoke hearts in oil, drained

4 small tomatoes

25 g/1 oz sun-dried tomatoes in oil, drained

40 g/1½ oz Parma ham

25 g/1 oz stoned black olives, halved

handful of fresh basil leaves

DRESSING

3 tbsp olive oil

1 tbsp white wine vinegar

1 garlic clove, crushed

½ tsp mild mustard

1 tsp clear honey

salt and pepper

USE BOTTLED ARTICHOKES IN OIL IF YOU CAN FIND THEM, AS THEY HAVE A BETTER FLAVOUR.

4

MAIN COURSES

Meat takes pride of place in this selection of classic dishes that are drawn from traditional cuisine around the world. You'll find plenty of ideas for everyday meals for friends and family and simple yet sophisticated dishes for when you want to entertain in style. If you're in the mood for Chicken with Saffron Mash or just a simple Grilled Steak, you'll find the recipe here. Venture further afield with Grecian Meatballs, Aromatic Duck or Puy Lentils with Sausage, or try out some Chicken Fajitas.

CHICKEN WITH SAFFRON MASH

Put the potatoes, garlic and saffron in a large, heavy-based saucepan, add the stock and bring to the boil. Reduce the heat, cover and simmer for 20 minutes, or until tender.

Meanwhile, brush the chicken breasts all over with half the oil and the lemon juice. Sprinkle with the chopped thyme, fresh coriander and crushed coriander seeds. Heat a griddle pan over a medium–high heat, add the chicken and cook for 5 minutes on each side, or until the juices run clear when a skewer is inserted into the thickest part of the meat. Alternatively, cook the chicken breasts under a preheated hot grill for 5 minutes on each side, or until cooked through.

Drain the potatoes and return the contents of the sieve to the saucepan. Add the remaining oil and the milk, season to taste with salt and pepper and mash until smooth.

Divide the saffron mash between 4 large, warmed serving plates, top with a cooked chicken breast and garnish with a few thyme sprigs. Serve immediately.

SERVES 4

550 g/1 lb 4 oz floury potatoes, cut into chunks

1 garlic clove, peeled and sliced

1 tsp saffron threads, crushed

1.2 litres/2 pints chicken or vegetable stock

4 skinless, boneless chicken breasts, about 115 g/4 oz each, trimmed of all visible fat

2 tbsp olive oil

1 tbsp lemon juice

1 tbsp chopped fresh thyme, plus extra sprigs to garnish

1 tbsp chopped fresh coriander

1 tbsp coriander seeds, crushed

100 ml/3$^{1}/_{2}$ fl oz hot skimmed milk

salt and pepper

CHICKEN FAJITAS

Put all the ingredients for the marinade in a large, shallow, non-metallic dish or bowl and mix together well.

Slice the chicken across the grain into slices 2.5 cm/1 inch thick. Toss in the marinade until well coated. Cover and leave to marinate in the refrigerator for 2–3 hours, turning occasionally.

Heat a griddle pan over a medium–high heat. Remove the chicken slices from the marinade with a slotted spoon, add to the griddle pan and cook for 3–4 minutes on each side until cooked through. Transfer to a warmed serving plate and keep warm.

Add the red peppers, skin-side down, to the griddle pan and cook for 2 minutes on each side. Transfer to the serving plate.

Pile the cooked chicken and peppers onto the warmed tortillas, along with some guacamole, soured cream, tomato salsa and shredded lettuce. Serve with refried beans or boiled rice, if you like.

SERVES 4

4 skinless, boneless chicken breasts, about 115 g/4 oz each

2 red peppers, deseeded and cut into 2.5-cm/1-inch strips

8 flour tortillas, warmed

ready-made guacamole

soured cream

tomato salsa

shredded iceberg lettuce

refried beans or boiled rice, to serve (optional)

MARINADE

3 tbsp olive oil, plus extra for drizzling

3 tbsp maple syrup or honey

1 tbsp red wine vinegar

2 garlic cloves, crushed

2 tsp dried oregano

1–2 tsp crushed dried red chillies

salt and pepper

GRILLED CHICKEN WITH LEMON

Prick the skin of the chicken quarters all over with a fork. Put the chicken in a non-metallic dish, add the lemon juice, oil, garlic, thyme and salt and pepper to taste and mix together well. Cover and leave to marinate in the refrigerator for at least 2 hours.

To cook the chicken, preheat the grill to medium. Put the chicken in the grill pan and baste with the marinade. Cook under the preheated grill, turning occasionally and basting with the marinade, but not for the last 10 minutes of the cooking time, for 30–40 minutes until the chicken is tender and the juices run clear when a skewer is inserted into the thickest part of the meat.

Serve hot, garnished with the lemon rind and a few thyme sprigs.

SERVES 4

4 chicken quarters

juice and grated rind of 2 lemons

4 tbsp olive oil

2 garlic cloves, crushed

2 fresh thyme sprigs, plus extra to garnish

salt and pepper

SERVES 6–8

2 pinches of saffron threads

4 tablespoons hot water

400 g/14 oz Spanish short-grain rice

16 live mussels

about 6 tbsp olive oil

6–8 unboned chicken thighs, skin on, excess fat removed

140 g/5 oz chorizo sausage, casing removed, cut into 5-mm/¼-inch slices

2 large onions, chopped

4 large garlic cloves, crushed

1 tsp mild or hot Spanish paprika, to taste

100 g/3½ oz French or other green beans, chopped

100 g/3½ oz frozen peas

1.2 litres/2 pints fish, chicken or vegetable stock

16 raw prawns, peeled and deveined

2 red peppers, grilled, peeled, deseeded and sliced

35 g/1¼ oz fresh parsley, finely chopped

salt and pepper

PAELLA WITH CHICKEN AND CHORIZO

Put the saffron threads and water in a small bowl and leave to soak. Put the rice in a sieve and rinse in cold water until the water runs clear. Set aside. Clean the mussels by scrubbing or scraping the shells and pulling out any beards that are attached to them. Discard any with broken shells or any that refuse to close when tapped. Set aside.

Heat 3 tablespoons of the oil in a 30-cm/12-inch paella pan or flameproof casserole over a medium–high heat. Add the chicken, skin-side down, and cook for 5 minutes, or until golden and crisp. Transfer to a bowl. Add the chorizo and cook for 1 minute, or until it starts to crisp. Add to the chicken.

Heat another 3 tablespoons of oil in the paella pan. Add the onions and cook, stirring, for 2 minutes, then add the garlic and paprika and cook, stirring, for a further 3 minutes until the onions are softened but not browned.

Add the drained rice, beans and peas and stir until coated in oil. Return the chicken thighs and chorizo and any accumulated juices

to the pan. Stir in the stock, saffron and its soaking liquid and salt and pepper to taste. Bring to the boil, stirring constantly.

Reduce the heat to low and simmer, without stirring, for 15 minutes, or until the rice is almost tender and most of the liquid is absorbed.

Arrange the mussels, prawns and pepper strips on top, cover the pan and simmer, without stirring, for a further 5 minutes, or until the prawns become pink and the mussels are opened.

Discard any mussels that remain closed. Taste and adjust the seasoning. Sprinkle with the parsley and serve immediately.

The first time you make this, preheat the oven to 190°C/375°F/Gas Mark 5 while the paella simmers. Heat sources are not consistent on hobs, so it is hard to say how long it takes for the liquid to be absorbed. If there is too much liquid on the surface, put the dish in the oven, cover and bake for 10 minutes, or until very little liquid remains.

CHICKEN WITH VEGETABLES AND CORIANDER RICE

Heat the oil in a preheated wok or large frying pan over a high heat. Add the onion, garlic and ginger and stir-fry for 1–2 minutes.

Add the chicken and mushrooms and stir-fry until the chicken is browned. Add the coconut milk, sugar snap peas, soy sauce and fish sauce and bring to the boil. Reduce the heat and simmer gently for 4–5 minutes until the chicken and vegetables are tender.

To make the rice, heat the oil in a separate preheated wok or large frying pan over a medium heat. Add the onion and stir-fry until softened but not browned. Add the cooked rice, pak choi and coriander and cook, stirring, until the leaves are wilted and the rice is thoroughly hot. Sprinkle over the soy sauce and serve immediately with the chicken.

SERVES 4

2 tbsp vegetable or groundnut oil

1 red onion, chopped

2 garlic cloves, chopped

2.5-cm/1-inch piece fresh root ginger, chopped

2 skinless, boneless chicken breasts, about 115 g/4 oz each, cut into strips

115 g/4 oz button mushrooms

400 g/14 oz canned coconut milk

55 g/2 oz sugar snap peas, halved lengthways

2 tbsp soy sauce

1 tbsp Thai fish sauce

RICE

1 tbsp vegetable or groundnut oil

1 red onion, sliced

350 g/12 oz rice, cooked and cooled

250 g/8 oz pak choi, torn into large pieces

handful of fresh coriander, chopped

2 tbsp Thai soy sauce

PARIKA CHICKEN ON A BED OF ONIONS AND HAM

Put the chicken in a non-metallic bowl. Pour over the lemon juice, cover and leave to marinate in the refrigerator overnight.

Remove the chicken from the marinade and pat dry with kitchen paper. Rub the skins with the paprika and salt and pepper to taste.

Heat 2 tablespoons oil in a large, heavy-based frying pan with a lid or flameproof casserole over a medium–high heat. Add the chicken breasts, skin-side down, and cook for 5 minutes, or until the skins are crisp and golden. Remove from the frying pan.

Stir the ham into the fat remaining in the frying pan, cover and cook for 2 minutes, or until the fat runs. Add the onions and cook, stirring occasionally and adding a little extra oil if necessary, for 5 minutes, or until the onions are softened but not browned.

Add the wine and stock and bring to the boil, stirring. Return the chicken breasts to the frying pan and season to taste with salt and pepper. Reduce the heat, cover and simmer for 20 minutes, or until the chicken is tender and the juices run clear when a skewer is inserted into the thickest part of the meat.

Transfer the chicken to a plate and keep warm in a low oven. Bring the sauce to the boil and cook until the juices have reduced. Taste and adjust the seasoning.

Divide the sauce between 4 individual warmed plates and arrange a chicken breast on top of each. Garnish with thyme sprigs and serve immediately.

SERVES 4

4 chicken breast fillets, about 115 g/4 oz each, skin on

150 ml/5 fl oz freshly squeezed lemon juice

1–1$\frac{1}{2}$ tsp mild or hot Spanish paprika, to taste

about 2 tbsp olive oil

70 g/2$\frac{1}{2}$ oz serrano ham, diced

4 large onions, thinly sliced

125 ml/4 fl oz dry white wine

125 ml/4 fl oz chicken stock

salt and pepper

fresh thyme sprigs, to garnish

AROMATIC DUCK

SERVES 6–8

1 duckling, weighing 2 kg/
4 lb 8 oz

1 tsp salt

8 slices fresh root ginger

3 spring onions

3 cloves

1 cinnamon stick

3 tbsp Shaoxing rice wine or
dry sherry

1 tsp sesame oil

1 tbsp light soy sauce

2 tsp dark soy sauce

25 g/1 oz rock sugar

250 ml/9 fl oz water

Rinse the duckling and pat dry with kitchen paper. Rub the skin with the salt and leave to stand for 15 minutes. Rinse well.

Stuff the duckling with the ginger and spring onions, then put in a flameproof casserole with all the remaining ingredients. Bring to the boil, then reduce the heat, cover and simmer for 1 hour.

Remove the duckling from the casserole and cut into chunks.

Transfer the duck pieces to a serving dish. Sieve the gravy, skimming off any fat, and pour it over the duck. Serve immediately.

ROCK SUGAR TYPICALLY COMES IN THE FORM OF TRANSPARENT BLOCKS THAT ARE AVAILABLE FROM CHINESE FOOD STORES.

DUCK BREASTS WITH FRUIT SAUCE

SERVES 4

4 boneless duck breasts, about
175 g/6 oz each, skin on

1 tbsp sunflower oil

125 ml/4 fl oz dry white wine

125 g/4^{1}/$_{2}$ oz frozen mixed
berries, straight from
the freezer, or fresh berries

1 tbsp clear honey

^{1}/$_{4}$ tsp ground mixed spice

salt and pepper

Preheat the oven to 200°C/400°F/
Gas Mark 6. Finely score each duck
breast in a criss-cross pattern
through the skin into the fat.

Heat the oil in a large sauté or
frying pan over a high heat. Add the
duck breasts, skin-side down, and
cook for 4 minutes, or until the skin
is crisp and golden brown. Using a
slotted spoon, transfer the duck
breasts to a roasting tin, skin-side
up, and roast in the preheated oven
for 12 minutes for medium-rare or
15 minutes for medium.

Meanwhile, tip the excess fat out
of the sauté pan. Put the pan over a
high heat, add the wine and bring to
the boil, scraping any sediment
from the base of the pan. Stir in the
fruit, reduce the heat to medium
and leave to simmer for 5 minutes,
or until tender, stirring occasionally
and pressing down with the back of
a wooden spoon.

Add the honey and mixed spice
and stir until the honey dissolves.
Season to taste with salt and
pepper and add extra honey or
spice, as desired. Reduce the heat to
low and leave the sauce to simmer
and reduce, stirring occasionally.

Transfer the duck breasts to a
carving board, cover loosely with foil
and leave to rest for a few minutes.
Thinly slice the duck breasts on the
diagonal and transfer to warmed
serving plates. Add any accumulated
duck juices to the sauce and adjust
the seasoning, if necessary.

At this point, the sauce can be
used as it is, containing pieces of
fruit, or processed in a food
processor or blender and passed
through a non-metallic sieve to
make a smooth sauce, reheating
if necessary.

Spoon the fruit sauce over the
duck breasts and serve immediately.

VEAL WITH PARMA HAM AND SAGE

Put the veal escalopes between 2 sheets of clingfilm and pound with the flat end of a meat mallet or with the side of a rolling pin until very thin. Transfer to a plate and sprinkle with the lemon juice. Cover and leave to marinate in the refrigerator for 30 minutes, spooning the lemon juice over occasionally.

Pat the escalopes dry with kitchen paper, season to taste with salt and pepper and rub with half the sage. Put a slice of ham on each escalope. Secure with a cocktail stick.

Melt the butter in a large, heavy-based frying pan over a low heat. Add the remaining sage and cook, stirring constantly, for 1 minute. Add the escalopes and cook for 3–4 minutes on each side until golden brown. Pour in the wine and cook for a further 2 minutes.

Transfer the escalopes to a warmed serving dish and pour over the pan juices. Remove and discard the cocktail sticks and serve the escalopes immediately.

SERVES 4

4 veal escalopes

2 tbsp lemon juice

1 tbsp chopped fresh sage leaves

4 slices Parma ham

55 g/2 oz unsalted butter

3 tbsp dry white wine

salt and pepper

YOU CAN ALSO PREPARE SKINNED, BONED CHICKEN BREASTS IN THE SAME WAY. IF THEY ARE VERY THICK, CUT THEM HORIZONTALLY IN HALF FIRST.

BRAISED VEAL IN RED WINE

Preheat the oven to 180°C/350°F/ Gas Mark 4. Put the flour and pepper to taste in a polythene bag, add the meat and shake well to coat each piece. Heat the oil in a large, flameproof casserole. Add the meat, in batches, and cook for 5–10 minutes, stirring constantly, until browned all over. Remove with a slotted spoon and set aside.

Add the whole onions, garlic and carrots to the casserole and cook, stirring frequently, for 5 minutes until beginning to soften.

Return the meat to the casserole. Pour in the wine, scraping any sediment from the base of the casserole, then add the stock, tomatoes with their juice, lemon rind, bay leaf, parsley, basil, thyme and salt and pepper to taste. Bring to the boil, then cover the casserole.

Transfer to the preheated oven and cook for 2 hours, or until the meat is tender.

Serve hot, garnished with extra chopped parsley and accompanied by boiled rice.

SERVES 6

25 g/1 oz plain flour

900 g/2 lb stewing veal or beef, cubed

4 tbsp olive oil

350 g/12 oz button onions

2 garlic cloves, finely chopped

350 g/12 oz carrots, sliced

300 ml/10 fl oz full-bodied red wine

150 ml/5 fl oz beef or chicken stock

400 g/14 oz canned chopped tomatoes with herbs in juice

pared rind of 1 lemon

1 bay leaf

1 tbsp chopped fresh flat-leaf parsley, plus extra to garnish

1 tbsp chopped fresh basil

1 tsp chopped fresh thyme

salt and pepper

boiled rice, to serve

GRILLED STEAK

To make the Maître d'Hôtel Butter, put the butter in a bowl and beat with a wooden spoon until softened. Add the parsley and lemon juice, season to taste with salt and pepper and beat together until thoroughly combined.

Turn out onto a sheet of greaseproof paper and shape into a roll. Wrap in the greaseproof paper and chill for 2–3 hours until firm. Just before serving, slice the butter into thin rounds.

Preheat the grill or barbecue. Brush each steak with oil and season to taste with pepper.

Put the steaks onto an oiled grill rack and cook under or over a medium heat for the required length of time and according to your taste: for 2-cm/³/₄-inch thick steaks, 5 minutes for rare, 8–10 minutes for medium and 12–14 minutes for well done; for 2.5-cm/1-inch thick steaks, 6–7 minutes for rare, 8–10 minutes for medium and 12–15 minutes for well done; for 4-cm/1¹/₂-inch thick steaks, 10 minutes for rare, 12–14 minutes for medium and 18–20 minutes for well done. During cooking, turn the steaks frequently, using a spatula rather than a sharp tool so that you don't pierce the meat and allow the juices to escape. When you turn the steaks, brush them once or twice with oil. Watch the steaks constantly during cooking to ensure that they don't overcook.

Serve immediately, with each steak topped with a slice of Maître d'Hôtel Butter and accompanied by a baked potato and green salad.

SERVES 6

6 rump, sirloin or fillet steaks, about 175–225 g/6–8 oz each

olive or sunflower oil, for brushing and oiling

pepper

MAITRE D'HOTEL BUTTER

115 g/4 oz butter

3 tbsp finely chopped fresh parsley

1 tbsp lemon juice

salt and pepper

TO SERVE

baked potatoes

green salad

IF THE STEAKS HAVE A PIECE OF FAT RUNNING ALONG THEM, CUT OR SNIP INTO IT AT REGULAR INTERVALS TO PREVENT THE STEAKS FROM CURLING DURING COOKING. A BAKED POTATO AND SALAD HAS BEEN SUGGESTED AS HEALTHY ACCOMPANIMENTS, BUT YOU COULD SERVE THE STEAKS WITH CHIPS AND BATTERED DEEP-FRIED ONION RINGS INSTEAD.

PEPPERED T-BONE STEAKS

SERVES 2

2 tbsp black peppercorns, green peppercorns or a mixture of both

2 T-bone steaks, about 250 g/ 9 oz each

2 tbsp butter

1 tbsp olive or sunflower oil

125 ml/4 fl oz red wine

salt

TO SERVE

green beans

long-grain rice, cooked with turmeric for added colour

Put the peppercorns in a mortar and roughly crush with a pestle. Alternatively, put in a strong polythene bag, put on a chopping board and roughly crush with the end of a rolling pin.

Spread the crushed peppercorns (removing the 'dust') out on a plate and press one side of each steak hard into them to encrust the surface of the meat. Turn the steak over and repeat with the other side.

Melt the butter with the oil in a large, heavy-based frying pan over a high heat. When hot, add the steaks and cook quickly on both sides to

seal. Reduce the heat to medium and cook, turning once, for 2$\frac{1}{2}$–3 minutes each side for rare, 3$\frac{1}{2}$–5 minutes each side for medium or 5–7 minutes each side for well done. Transfer the steaks to warmed plates and keep warm.

Add the wine to the frying pan and stir, scraping any sediment from the base of the frying pan. Bring to the boil and continue to boil until reduced by about half. Season to taste with salt.

Pour the pan juices over the steaks and serve immediately with green beans and rice.

BAKED PASTA WITH SPICY MEAT SAUCE

Preheat the oven to 190°C/375°F/ Gas Mark 5. Heat the oil in a saucepan over a medium heat. Add the onion and garlic and cook, stirring frequently, for 5 minutes, or until the onion is softened. Add the mince and cook, stirring constantly with a wooden spoon to break up the meat, for 5 minutes, or until browned all over.

Add the tomatoes with their juice, sugar, herbs, spices and salt and pepper to taste. Bring to the boil, then reduce the heat and simmer, uncovered, for 30 minutes, stirring occasionally.

Meanwhile, cook the pasta in a large saucepan of boiling salted water for 10–12 minutes, or according to the packet instructions, until tender but still firm to the bite. Drain well. Beat the eggs, yogurt, feta cheese and salt and pepper to taste together in a bowl.

Transfer the meat mixture to a large ovenproof dish. Add the pasta in a layer to cover the meat, then pour over the yogurt mixture. Sprinkle over the pecorino cheese.

Bake in the preheated oven for 30–45 minutes until golden brown. Serve hot or warm.

SERVES 4–6

2 tbsp olive oil

1 onion, finely chopped

2 garlic cloves, finely chopped

650 g/1 lb 7 oz lean fresh lamb or beef mince

400 g/14 oz canned chopped tomatoes in juice

pinch of sugar

2 tbsp chopped fresh flat-leaf parsley

1 tbsp chopped fresh marjoram

1 tsp ground cinnamon

$1/2$ tsp freshly grated nutmeg

$1/4$ tsp ground cloves

225 g/8 oz dried macaroni or other short pasta

2 eggs, beaten

300 ml/10 fl oz Greek yogurt

55 g/2 oz feta cheese (drained weight), grated

25 g/1 oz pecorino cheese, grated

salt and pepper

SPAGHETTI AND MEATBALLS

SERVES 6

25 g/1 oz white bread, crusts removed, torn into pieces

2 tbsp milk

450 g/1 lb fresh beef mince

4 tbsp chopped fresh flat-leaf parsley

1 egg

pinch of cayenne pepper

2 tbsp olive oil

150 ml/5 fl oz passata

200 g/7 oz canned chopped tomatoes in juice

400 ml/14 fl oz vegetable stock

pinch of sugar

450 g/1 lb dried spaghetti

salt and pepper

Put the bread in a small bowl, add the milk and leave to soak. Meanwhile, put the mince in a large bowl and add half the parsley, the egg and the cayenne pepper. Season to taste with salt and pepper. Squeeze the excess moisture out of the bread and crumble it over the meat mixture. Mix together well until smooth.

Shape small pieces of the mixture into balls between the palms of your hands and put on a baking sheet or chopping board. Cover and chill for 30 minutes.

Heat the oil in a heavy-based frying pan. Add the meatballs, in batches, and cook, turning frequently, until browned all over. Return all the meatballs to the frying pan, add the passata, tomatoes with their juice, stock and sugar and season to taste with salt and pepper. Bring to the boil, stirring, then reduce the heat, cover and leave to simmer for 25–30 minutes until the sauce is thickened and the meatballs are tender and cooked through.

Meanwhile, bring a large saucepan of lightly salted water to the boil. Add the pasta, return to the boil and cook for 8–10 minutes, or according to the packet instructions, until tender but still firm to the bite. Drain and transfer to a warmed serving dish. Pour over the sauce and toss lightly. Sprinkle with the remaining parsley and serve.

WHEN FORMING THE MEAT MIXTURE INTO BALLS, DAMPEN YOUR HANDS SLIGHTLY WITH A LITTLE COLD WATER TO HELP PREVENT THE MIXTURE STICKING.

PORK STIR-FRY

Mix the soy sauce, rice wine, vinegar, sugar and five-spice powder together in a small bowl. Drain the pineapple, reserving the juice in a jug. Chop the pineapple and reserve until required. Stir the cornflour into the pineapple juice until a smooth paste forms, then stir the paste into the soy sauce mixture and reserve.

Heat the oil in a preheated wok or large, heavy-based frying pan over a high heat. Add the spring onions, garlic and ginger and stir-fry for 30 seconds. Add the pork strips and stir-fry for 3 minutes, or until browned all over.

Add the carrots, baby sweetcorn and green pepper and stir-fry for 3 minutes. Add the beansprouts and mangetout and stir-fry for 2 minutes. Add the pineapple and the soy sauce mixture and cook, stirring constantly, for a further 2 minutes, or until slightly thickened.

Transfer to warmed serving bowls and serve immediately.

SERVES 4

2 tbsp dark soy sauce

1 tbsp Shaoxing rice wine or dry sherry

1 tbsp rice vinegar

1 tbsp soft light brown sugar

1 tsp Chinese five-spice powder

225 g/8 oz canned pineapple rings in juice

1 tbsp cornflour

1 tbsp groundnut oil

4 spring onions, chopped

1 garlic clove, finely chopped

2.5-cm/1-inch piece fresh root ginger, finely chopped

350 g/12 oz pork loin, cut into very thin strips

3 carrots, cut into thin batons

175 g/6 oz baby sweetcorn

1 green pepper, deseeded and thinly sliced

115 g/4 oz fresh beansprouts

115 g/4 oz mangetout

PUY LENTILS WITH SAUSAGES

SERVES 4–6

2 tbsp sunflower oil, plus extra for brushing

1 large onion, finely chopped

2 large garlic cloves, finely chopped

2 carrots, cut into 5-mm/ $^1/_4$-inch dice

400 g/14 oz Puy lentils, rinsed

$^1/_2$ tsp dried thyme

1 bay leaf

4–12 fresh sausages, such as Toulouse

2 tbsp chopped fresh flat-leaf parsley

salt and pepper

VINAIGRETTE

60 ml/2 fl oz walnut oil

$4^1/_2$ tsp white wine vinegar or lemon juice

$^1/_2$ tsp Dijon mustard

$^1/_4$ tsp caster sugar

salt and pepper

To make the Vinaigrette, put all ingredients in a jar, then blend using a stick blender until a thick emulsion forms. Alternatively, put all the ingredients in a screw-top jar, secure the lid and shake vigorously until the emulsion forms. Taste and adjust the seasoning if necessary, and set aside.

Heat the oil in a heavy-based saucepan with a tight-fitting lid over a medium–high heat. Add the onion, garlic and carrots and cook, stirring frequently, for 5 minutes, or until the onion is softened but not browned.

Stir in the lentils. Add enough water to cover the lentils by 2.5 cm/1 inch and bring to the boil, skimming the surface with a spoon, if necessary. Stir in the thyme and bay leaf, then reduce the heat to low, cover and leave to simmer for 10 minutes.

Uncover the saucepan and simmer for a further 15–20 minutes, or until the carrots and lentils are tender. If the water is absorbed before the lentils are tender, add a little more and continue cooking.

Meanwhile, preheat the grill to high. Brush the grill rack with oil. Lightly prick the sausages all over and cook under the preheated grill, turning occasionally, until cooked through and the skins are crisp and brown. Set aside and keep warm.

The lentils should absorb all the water by the time they are tender, but if any remains on the surface, drain it off. Transfer the lentils to a large serving bowl. Add the vinaigrette to the hot lentils and stir so that they are well coated.

Add salt and pepper to taste, then stir in the parsley. Serve the hot lentils with the sausages.

GRIDDLED PORK WITH ORANGE SAUCE

Mix the orange juice, vinegar and garlic together in a shallow, non-metallic dish and season to taste with pepper. Add the pork and turn to coat in the marinade. Cover and leave to marinate in the refrigerator for up to 3 hours.

Meanwhile, mix all the ingredients for the gremolata together in a small bowl, cover and chill until required.

Heat a non-stick griddle pan over a medium–high heat and brush lightly with oil. Remove the pork from the marinade – reserving the marinade – add to the griddle pan and cook for 5 minutes on each side, or until cooked through.

Meanwhile, pour the marinade into a small saucepan, bring to the boil and boil for 5 minutes, or until slightly thickened.

Transfer the pork to a serving dish, pour the orange sauce over and sprinkle with the gremolata. Serve immediately.

SERVES 4

4 tbsp freshly squeezed orange juice

4 tbsp red wine vinegar

2 garlic cloves, finely chopped

4 pork steaks, trimmed of all visible fat

olive oil, for brushing

pepper

GREMOLATA

3 tbsp finely chopped fresh parsley

grated rind of 1 lime

grated rind of $^{1}/_{2}$ lemon

1 garlic clove, very finely chopped

THIS DISH WOULD WORK EQUALLY WELL WITH CHICKEN BREAST PORTIONS. REMOVE THE SKIN FROM THE COOKED CHICKEN BEFORE SERVING.

SWEET AND SOUR GLAZED PORK

Preheat the oven to 230°C/450°F/ Gas Mark 8. To make the stuffing, melt the butter in a saucepan over a medium heat. Add the onion and cook, stirring, for 3 minutes, or until slightly softened. Add the mushrooms and cook, stirring, for 2 minutes. Remove from the heat and stir in the breadcrumbs, chopped sage, lemon juice and salt and pepper to taste.

Put the stuffing in the middle of the pork loin, then roll up and secure with several lengths of string tied around the loin. Put the joint in a roasting tin, rub the skin with plenty of salt and season to taste with pepper. Mix the honey, vinegar, soy sauce and mustard together in a small bowl. Pour the mixture over the pork.

Cook in the preheated oven for 20 minutes, then reduce the heat to 180°C/350°F/Gas Mark 4 and cook, basting occasionally, for 1¼ hours, or until tender and cooked through.

Remove from the oven and leave to rest for 15 minutes. Garnish with sage sprigs and serve with roasted root vegetables.

SERVES 4

1 kg/2 lb 4 oz pork loin, backbone removed and rind scored

6 tbsp clear honey

1 tbsp wine vinegar

1 tsp soy sauce

1 tsp Dijon mustard

salt and pepper

roasted root vegetables, to serve

STUFFING

6 tbsp butter

1 onion, chopped

100 g/3½ oz button mushrooms, chopped

100 g/3½ oz fresh breadcrumbs

2 tbsp finely chopped fresh sage, plus extra sprigs to garnish

1 tbsp lemon juice

salt and pepper

KIDNEYS IN MUSTARD SAUCE

Using a pair of kitchen scissors, remove the cores from the kidneys and discard. Melt the butter with the oil in a large sauté or frying pan over a medium–high heat. Add the kidney halves, in batches if necessary, and cook, turning occasionally, for 3 minutes, or until browned all over. Using a slotted spoon, transfer the kidney halves to a plate, then cover with foil, shiny-side down, set aside and keep warm.

Add the shallots and garlic to the fat in the pan and cook, stirring, for 2 minutes, or until the shallots are softened but not browned. Add the wine, bring to the boil and boil until reduced by half, scraping the sediment from the base of the pan.

Add the stock, return to the boil and boil again until reduced by half. Stir in the cream and mustard, reduce the heat to medium–low and return the kidneys to the pan. Cover and simmer for 5 minutes, or until the kidneys are cooked through.

Remove the kidneys from the pan and keep warm. Increase the heat under the sauce and leave to bubble until reduced and thickened.

Add salt and pepper to taste, return the kidneys to the pan and stir well. Garnish with chopped parsley and serve immediately.

SERVES 4–6

12 lamb's kidneys, skinned and halved

25 g/1 oz unsalted butter

1 tbsp sunflower oil

2 large shallots, chopped

1 garlic clove, very finely chopped

2 tbsp dry white wine

125 ml/4 fl oz chicken or lamb stock

250 ml/9 oz double cream

2 tbsp Dijon mustard, or to taste

salt and pepper

chopped fresh flat-leaf parsley, to garnish

LAMB'S LIVER IN RED WINE AND ORANGE SAUCE

Using a zester, remove the zest from the oranges. Put the zest in a small saucepan of boiling water, boil for 1 minute, then drain and set aside. Squeeze the juice from the oranges and set aside.

Remove and discard any ducts and membrane from the liver slices. Put the flour and paprika in a polythene bag, add the liver and shake well to coat each piece.

Heat the oil in a large frying pan over a medium heat. Add the liver and cook, stirring constantly, for 4–5 minutes until lightly browned all over but still moist in the centre.

Remove from the frying pan with a slotted spoon and divide between 4 warmed serving plates on a bed of cooked pasta.

Add the wine to the frying pan, scraping any sediment from the base of the pan. Boil briskly for 1 minute. Reduce the heat and stir in the orange juice, parsley, oregano and salt and pepper to taste. Cook gently until slightly reduced, then spoon over the liver and garnish with the reserved orange zest and parsley. Serve immediately.

SERVES 4

2 oranges

8 thin slices lamb's or calf's liver

2 tbsp plain flour

1 tsp paprika

3 tbsp olive oil

175 ml/6 fl oz full-bodied red wine

2 tbsp chopped fresh flat-leaf parsley, plus extra to garnish

2 tbsp chopped fresh oregano

salt and pepper

cooked pasta, to serve

MINTY LAMB BURGERS

Preheat the grill to medium. Put the peppers, onion and aubergine on the grill rack, brush the aubergine with 1 tablespoon of the oil and cook under the preheated grill for 10–12 minutes, or until charred. Remove from the grill, leave to cool, then peel the peppers. Put all the vegetables in a food processor and pulse until chopped.

Add the mince, Parmesan cheese, mint and salt and pepper to taste to the food processor and process until the mixture comes together. Scrape onto a chopping board. With damp hands, shape the mixture into 4–6 equal-sized burgers. Cover and chill for at least 30 minutes.

Mix together the mayonnaise ingredients. Preheat the grill to medium. Lightly brush the burgers with the remaining oil and cook under the preheated grill for 3–4 minutes on each side. Serve the burgers on a bed of lettuce on the bases of the baps. Spoon the mayonnaise on top of each burger and place the lids in position.

SERVES 4–6

1 red pepper, deseeded and cut into quarters

1 yellow pepper, deseeded and cut into quarters

1 red onion, cut into thick wedges

1 baby aubergine, about 115 g/ 4 oz, cut into wedges

2 tbsp olive oil

450 g/1 lb fresh lamb mince

2 tbsp freshly grated Parmesan cheese

1 tbsp chopped fresh mint

salt and pepper

MAYONNAISE

4 tbsp mayonnaise

1 tsp Dijon mustard

1 tbsp chopped fresh mint

TO SERVE

4–6 toasted sesame seed baps

lettuce leaves, shredded

GRECIAN MEATBALLS

Put the mince in a bowl. Grate in the onion, then add the garlic, breadcrumbs, mint and parsley. Season well with salt and pepper. Mix the ingredients together well, then add the egg and mix to bind the mixture together.

Alternatively, the ingredients for the meatballs can be combined in a food processor.

Preheat the grill to medium. With damp hands, shape the mixture into 16 equal-sized balls and thread onto 4 flat metal skewers.

Lightly oil a grill pan and brush the meatballs with oil.

Cook the meatballs under the preheated grill, turning frequently and brushing with more oil if necessary, for 10 minutes, or until cooked through and browned.

SERVES 4

450 g/1 lb fine lean fresh lamb mince

1 onion

1 garlic clove, crushed

25 g/1 oz fresh white or brown breadcrumbs

1 tbsp chopped fresh mint

1 tbsp chopped fresh parsley

1 egg, beaten

olive oil, for brushing

salt and pepper

LAMB SHANKS WITH ROASTED ONIONS

Preheat the oven to 180°C/350°F/ Gas Mark 4. Trim off any excess fat from the lamb shanks. Using a small, sharp knife, make 6 cuts in each lamb shank. Cut the garlic cloves lengthways into 4 slices. Insert 6 garlic slices into the cuts in each lamb shank.

Put the lamb in a single layer in a roasting tin, drizzle with the oil, sprinkle with the rosemary and season to taste with pepper. Roast in the preheated oven for 45 minutes.

Wrap each of the onions in a piece of foil. Remove the roasting tin from the oven and season the lamb to taste with salt. Return to the oven and put the wrapped onions on the shelf next to it. Roast for a further 1–1$\frac{1}{4}$ hours until the lamb is very tender.

Meanwhile, bring a large saucepan of water to the boil. Add the carrot batons and blanch for 1 minute. Drain and refresh in cold water.

Remove the roasting tin from the oven when the lamb is meltingly tender and transfer to a warmed serving dish. Skim off any fat from the roasting tin and put the tin over a medium heat. Add the carrots and cook, stirring, for 2 minutes, then add the water and bring to the boil. Reduce the heat and simmer, stirring constantly and scraping any sediment from the base of the tin.

Transfer the carrots and sauce to the serving dish. Remove the onions from the oven and unwrap. Cut off and discard about 1 cm/$\frac{1}{2}$ inch of the tops and add the onions to the serving dish. Serve immediately.

SERVES 4

4 lamb shanks, about 350 g/ 12 oz each

6 garlic cloves

2 tbsp virgin olive oil

1 tbsp fresh rosemary, very finely chopped

4 red onions

350 g/12 oz carrots, cut into thin batons

4 tbsp water

salt and pepper

5

ROASTS

Few meals are more satisfying than a good roast. The age-old ritual of carving a roast for family and friends is the epitome of what meat-eating is all about, incorporating a sociable occasion with the taste of traditional comfort food. Roasting is the easiest way of cooking meat, but it does call for top-quality produce, and it's absolutely vital to let the meat rest for at least 15 minutes before carving it – the meat will be juicier and more tender as a result. You'll find ideas for roasting all types of meat, poultry or game, including Roast Pork with Crackling, Roast Turkey with Bread Sauce and Quails with Grapes, or you can try out a new take on an old favourite, such as Roast Chicken Breasts with Bread Triangles or Roast Lamb with Orzo.

ROAST CHICKEN

SERVES 6

1 free-range chicken, weighing
2.25 kg/5 lb

55 g/2 oz butter

2 tbsp chopped fresh lemon
thyme, plus 6 extra sprigs
to garnish

1 lemon, quartered

125 ml/4 fl oz dry white wine

salt and pepper

Preheat the oven to 220°C/425°F/
Gas Mark 7. Wipe the chicken inside
and out with kitchen paper and put
in a roasting tin.

Put the butter in a bowl and
soften with a fork, then mix in the
thyme and season well with salt
and pepper. Spread the chicken all
over with the herb butter, inside
and out, and put the lemon quarters
inside the body cavity. Pour the
wine over the chicken.

Roast the chicken in the centre of
the preheated oven for 20 minutes.
Reduce the temperature to

190°C/375°F/Gas Mark 5 and roast,
basting frequently, for a further
1$\frac{1}{4}$ hours, or until tender and the
juices run clear when a skewer is
inserted into the thickest part of
the meat. Cover with foil if the skin
begins to brown too much. If the
roasting tin begins to dry out, add a
little more wine or water.

Transfer the chicken to a warmed
serving plate and leave to rest,
covered loosely with foil, for at least
15 minutes before carving.

Put the roasting tin on the hob
over a low heat and cook the pan
juices until reduced, thickened and
glossy. Season to taste with salt
and pepper.

Serve the roast chicken with the
pan juices, garnished with the
lemon thyme sprigs.

SIMPLY ROASTED, WITH LOTS OF THYME AND LEMON,
CHICKEN PRODUCES A SUCCULENT GASTRONOMIC
FEAST FOR MANY OCCASIONS. TRY TO BUY A GOOD
FRESH CHICKEN, AS FROZEN BIRDS DO NOT HAVE AS
MUCH FLAVOUR. YOU CAN STUFF YOUR CHICKEN
WITH A TRADITIONAL STUFFING, SUCH AS SAGE AND
ONION, OR FRUIT SUCH AS APRICOTS AND PRUNES,
BUT OFTEN THE BEST WAY IS TO KEEP IT SIMPLE.

ROAST CHICKEN BREASTS WITH BREAD TRIANGLES

Preheat the oven to 200°C/400°F/Gas Mark 6. Melt the butter in a saucepan over a medium heat, add the lemon juice, cranberries, sugar and salt and pepper to taste. Cook, stirring gently, for 1 minute and leave to cool until required.

Meanwhile, season the chicken to taste with salt and pepper. Wrap 2 bacon rashers around each breast and sprinkle with thyme.

Wrap each breast in a piece of lightly greased foil and put in a roasting tin. Roast in the preheated oven for 15 minutes. Remove the foil and roast the chicken breasts for a further 10 minutes.

Heat the dripping in a frying pan over a medium–high heat. Add the bread triangles and cook on both sides until golden brown.

Put a fried bread triangle on each individual warmed serving plate and top each with a chicken breast.

Serve immediately with a spoonful of the fruit sauce.

SERVES 8

55 g/2 oz butter, plus extra for greasing

juice of 1 lemon

250 g/9 oz cranberries or redcurrants

1–2 tbsp muscovado sugar

8 skinless chicken breasts

16 streaky bacon rashers

4 tsp dried thyme

55 g/2 oz beef dripping

4 slices bread, cut into triangles

salt and pepper

QUAILS WITH GRAPES

Preheat the oven to 230°C/450°F/ Gas Mark 8. Cook the potatoes for the pancake in a large saucepan of lightly salted water for 10 minutes until partially cooked. Drain and leave to cool completely, then peel, coarsely grate and season to taste with salt and pepper. Set aside.

Heat the oil in a heavy-based frying pan or flameproof casserole large enough to hold the quails in a single layer over a medium heat. Add the quails and cook, turning frequently, until golden brown all over.

Add the grapes, grape juice, cloves, enough water to come halfway up the sides of the quails, and salt and pepper to taste. Cover and simmer for 20 minutes. Transfer the quails and all the pan juices to a roasting tin, unless using a casserole, and sprinkle with brandy. Roast, uncovered, in the preheated

oven for 10 minutes. Meanwhile, to make the potato pancake, melt the butter with the oil in a 30-cm/ 12-inch non-stick frying pan over a high heat. When the fat is hot, add the potato and spread into an even layer. Reduce the heat and cook gently for 10 minutes.

Put a plate over the frying pan and, wearing oven gloves, invert both together so that the potato pancake drops onto the plate. Slide the potato back into the frying pan and cook for a further 10 minutes, or until cooked through and crisp. Slide out of the frying pan and cut into 4 wedges. Keep warm until the quails are ready.

To serve, put a potato pancake wedge and 2 quails on each warmed serving plate. Taste the grape sauce and adjust the seasoning, if necessary. Spoon over the quails and serve immediately.

SERVES 4

4 tbsp olive oil

8 oven-ready quails

280 g/10 oz green seedless grapes

225 ml/8 fl oz grape juice

2 cloves

about 150 ml/5 fl oz water

2 tbsp brandy

salt and pepper

POTATO PANCAKE

600 g/1 lb 5 oz unpeeled potatoes

35 g/1¼ oz unsalted butter or pork fat

1½ tbsp olive oil

BONED AND STUFFED ROAST DUCKLING

Preheat the oven to 190°C/375°F/ Gas Mark 5. Wipe the duckling inside and out with kitchen paper. Lay, skin-side down, on a chopping board and season well with salt and pepper.

Mix the sausage meat, onion, apple, apricots, walnuts and parsley together in a bowl. Season well with salt and pepper. Form into a large sausage shape.

Lay the duck breast(s) on the whole duckling and cover with the stuffing. Wrap the duckling around the stuffing and carefully tuck in any leg and neck flaps. Sew the duckling up the back and across

both ends with fine string. Try to use one piece of string so that you can remove it in one go. Mould the duckling into a good shape and put, sewn-side down, on a wire rack set over a roasting tin.

Roast in the preheated oven, basting occasionally and pouring off some of the fat in the tin, for 1½–2 hours until golden brown and crisp and the juices run clear when a skewer is inserted into the thickest part of the meat.

Simmer all the sauce ingredients in a saucepan for 2–3 minutes. Serve with the thickly sliced duck.

SERVES 6–8

1 duckling, weighing 1.8 kg/4 lb (dressed weight); ask your butcher to bone the duckling and cut off the wings at the first joint

450 g/1 lb herb-flavoured sausage meat

1 small onion, finely chopped

1 apple, cored and finely chopped

85 g/3 oz ready-to-eat dried apricots, finely chopped

85 g/3 oz chopped walnuts

2 tbsp chopped fresh parsley

1 large or 2 smaller duck breasts, skin removed

salt and pepper

APRICOT SAUCE

400 g/14 oz canned apricot halves in syrup, puréed with the syrup in a food processor or blender

150 ml/5 fl oz stock

125 ml/4 fl oz Marsala

½ tsp ground cinnamon

½ tsp ground ginger

salt and pepper

GUINEA FOWL WITH CABBAGE

Preheat the oven to 240°C/475°F/ Gas Mark 9. Rub the guinea fowl with the oil and season to taste inside and out with salt and pepper. Put the apple and parsley sprigs in the cavity and truss to tie the legs together. Put in a roasting tin and roast in the preheated oven for 20 minutes, or until the breast is golden brown. Immediately reduce the temperature to 160°C/325°F/ Gas Mark 3.

Meanwhile, blanch the cabbage in boiling water for 3 minutes. Drain, rinse in cold water and pat dry.

Put the lardons in a flameproof casserole over a medium–high heat and cook until the fat runs. Remove with a slotted spoon and set aside. Add the onion and cook, stirring frequently, for 5 minutes, or until softened but not browned. Add the bouquet garni with a very little salt and a pinch of pepper, then return the lardons to the casserole with the cabbage. Top with the guinea fowl. Cover with a piece of wet greaseproof paper, then add the lid and cook in the preheated oven for 45–60 minutes, or until the guinea fowl is tender and the juices run clear when a skewer is inserted into the thickest part of the meat.

Cut the guinea fowl into portions. Stir the parsley into the cabbage and onion and serve with the meat.

SERVES 4

1 oven-ready guinea fowl, weighing 1.25 kg/2 lb 12 oz

$^1/_2$ tbsp sunflower oil

$^1/_2$ apple, peeled, cored and chopped

several fresh flat-leaf parsley sprigs, stems bruised

1 large Savoy cabbage, coarse outer leaves discarded, cored and quartered

1 thick piece smoked belly of pork, about 140 g/5 oz, rind removed, cut into thin lardons, or 140 g/5 oz unsmoked lardons

1 onion, sliced

1 bouquet garni

$1^1/_2$ tbsp chopped fresh flat-leaf parsley

salt and pepper

IT IS IMPORTANT NOT TO ADD TOO MUCH SALT AS THE LARDONS WILL BE SALTY.

ROAST PHEASANT WITH RED WINE AND HERBS

SERVES 4

100 g/3$^1/_2$ oz butter, slightly softened

1 tbsp chopped fresh thyme

1 tbsp chopped fresh parsley

2 oven-ready young pheasants

4 tbsp vegetable oil

125 ml/4 fl oz full-bodied red wine

salt and pepper

good-quality, hand-fried crisps, to garnish

selection of vegetables, to serve

Preheat the oven to 190°C/375°F/ Gas Mark 5. Put the butter in a bowl and soften with a fork, then mix in the herbs. Lift the skins away from the pheasants, taking care not to tear them, and push the herb butter under the skins. Season to taste all over with salt and pepper.

Pour the oil into a roasting tin, add the pheasants and roast in the preheated oven for 45 minutes, basting occasionally. Remove from the oven, pour over the wine, then return to the oven and roast for a further 15 minutes, or until tender and the juices run clear when a skewer is inserted into the thickest part of the meat of both birds.

Remove the pheasants from the oven, cover loosely with foil and leave to rest for 15 minutes.

Transfer to a warmed serving platter and garnish with the crisps, known as game chips. To serve, cut the pheasants into portions and accompany with vegetables.

YULETIDE GOOSE
WITH HONEY AND PEARS

SERVES 4

1 oven-ready goose, weighing
3.5–4.5 kg/7 lb 12 oz–10 lb

1 tsp salt

4 pears

1 tbsp lemon juice

55 g/2 oz butter

2 tbsp clear honey

selection of vegetables, to serve

Preheat the oven to 220°C/425°F/ Gas Mark 7. Rinse the goose and pat dry with kitchen paper. Prick the skin all over with a fork, then rub with the salt. Put the bird upside down on a rack set over a roasting tin. Roast in the preheated oven for 30 minutes. Drain off the fat. Turn the bird over and roast for a further 15 minutes. Drain off the fat. Reduce the temperature to 180°C/350°F/ Gas Mark 4. Roast for a further 15 minutes per 450 g/1 lb, or until the juices run clear when a skewer is inserted into the thickest part of the meat. Cover with foil 15 minutes before the end of the cooking time.

Peel and halve the pears and brush with the lemon juice. Melt the butter and honey in a saucepan over a low heat, then add the pears. Cook, stirring, for 5–10 minutes until tender. Arrange around the goose on a serving platter and pour the sweet juices over the bird. Serve with a selection of vegetables.

GOOSE FAT IS SIMPLY PERFECT FOR ROASTING (AND SAUTÉEING) POTATOES, SO DON'T WASTE IT. POUR ANY THAT YOU ARE NOT ABOUT TO USE IMMEDIATELY INTO A SCREW-TOP JAR AND STORE IN THE REFRIGERATOR.

ROAST TURKEY WITH BREAD SAUCE

SERVES 8

1 quantity Chestnut and Sausage Stuffing

1 turkey, weighing 5 kg/11 lb

55 g/2 oz butter

5 tbsp full-bodied red wine

400 ml/14 fl oz chicken stock

1 tbsp cornflour

1 tsp French mustard

1 tsp sherry vinegar

2 teaspoons water

BREAD SAUCE

1 onion, peeled

4 cloves

600 ml/1 pint milk

115 g/4 oz fresh white breadcrumbs

55 g/2 oz butter

salt and pepper

Preheat the oven to 220°C/425°F/Gas Mark 7. Spoon the stuffing into the neck cavity of the turkey and close the flap of skin with a skewer. Put the bird in a large roasting tin and rub all over with 40 g/1½ oz of the butter. Roast in the preheated oven for 1 hour, then reduce the temperature to 180°C/350°F/Gas Mark 4 and roast for a further 2½ hours, or until tender and the juices run clear when a skewer is inserted into the thickest part of the meat. You may need to pour off the fat from the roasting tin occasionally.

Meanwhile, to make the bread sauce, stud the onion with the cloves, then put in a saucepan with the milk, breadcrumbs and butter. Bring just to boiling point over a low heat, then remove from the heat and leave to stand in a warm place to infuse.

Just before serving, remove the onion and reheat the sauce over a low heat, beating well with a wooden spoon. Season to taste with salt and pepper.

When the turkey is cooked, transfer to a carving board, cover loosely with foil and leave to rest.

To make the gravy, skim off the fat from the roasting tin, then place the tin over a medium heat. Add the wine and stir, scraping the sediment from the base of the tin. Stir in the stock. Mix the cornflour, mustard, vinegar and water together in a small bowl, then stir into the tin. Bring to the boil, stirring constantly, and cook until thickened and smooth. Add the remaining butter.

Carve the turkey and serve with the warm bread sauce and all the trimmings – including stuffing, roast potatoes and gravy.

ROAST PORK WITH CRACKLING

Preheat the oven to 200°C/400°F/ Gas Mark 6.

Score the pork rind thoroughly with a sharp knife and sprinkle with salt. Put it on a wire rack set over a baking tray and roast in the preheated oven for 30–40 minutes until the crackling is golden brown and crisp. This can be cooked in advance, leaving room in the oven for roast potatoes.

Season the pork well with salt and pepper and spread the fat with the mustard. Put in a roasting tin and roast in the centre of the oven for 20 minutes. Reduce the temperature to 190°C/375°F/ Gas Mark 5 and cook for a further 50–60 minutes until the meat is well browned and the juices run clear when a skewer is inserted into the thickest part of the meat.

Remove the meat from the oven and transfer to a warmed serving plate, cover loosely with foil and leave in a warm place to rest.

Meanwhile, to make the apple sauce, put all the ingredients into a saucepan over a low heat. Cook for 10 minutes, stirring occasionally. Beat well until the sauce is thick and smooth – use a hand-held electric whisk for a smooth finish.

To make the gravy, pour off most of the fat from the roasting tin, leaving the meat juices and the sediment. Put the tin over a medium heat and scrape the sediment from the base of the tin. Sprinkle in the flour and quickly whisk it into the juices. When you have a smooth paste, gradually add the cider, whisking constantly. Bring to the boil, then reduce the heat and simmer for 2–3 minutes until thickened. Season well with salt and pepper and pour into a warmed serving jug.

Carve the pork into slices and serve on warmed plates with pieces of the crackling and the gravy. Accompany with the apple sauce.

SERVES 4

1 boned pork loin joint, weighing 1 kg/2 lb 4 oz, rind removed and reserved

2 tbsp mustard

salt and pepper

APPLE SAUCE

450 g/1 lb Bramley apples, peeled, cored and sliced

3 tablespoons water

15 g/$\frac{1}{2}$ oz caster sugar

pinch of ground cinnamon (optional)

15 g/$\frac{1}{2}$ oz butter (optional)

GRAVY

1 tbsp flour

300 ml/10 fl oz cider, apple juice or chicken stock

salt and pepper

GLAZED HAM

Put the gammon in a large saucepan and add enough cold water to cover. Bring to the boil and skim off the scum that rises to the surface. Reduce the heat and simmer for 30 minutes.

Drain the gammon and return to the saucepan. Add the apple, onion, cider, peppercorns, bouquet garni, bay leaf and a few of the cloves. Pour in enough fresh water to cover and return to the boil. Reduce the heat, cover and simmer for 3 hours 20 minutes.

Preheat the oven to 200°C/400°F/ Gas Mark 6. Remove from the heat and leave to cool slightly. Remove the gammon from the cooking liquid and, while it is still warm, loosen the rind with a sharp knife, then peel it off and discard. Score the fat into diamond shapes and stud with the remaining cloves. Put the gammon on a rack set over a roasting tin and sprinkle with the sugar. Roast in the preheated oven, basting occasionally with the cooking liquid, for 20 minutes. Serve hot, or cold later.

SERVES 8

1 gammon joint, weighing 4 kg/9 lb

1 apple, cored and chopped

1 onion, chopped

300 ml/10 fl oz cider

6 black peppercorns

1 bouquet garni

1 bay leaf

about 50 cloves

4 tbsp demerara sugar

PORK WITH RED CABBAGE

Preheat the oven to 160°C/325°F/ Gas Mark 3. Heat the oil in a flameproof casserole over a medium heat. Add the pork and cook until browned all over. Transfer to a plate.

Add the onion and cook over a low heat, stirring occasionally, for 5 minutes, or until softened. Add the cabbage, in batches, and cook, stirring, for 2 minutes. Transfer each batch (mixed with some onion) into a bowl with a slotted spoon.

Add the apples, cloves and sugar to the bowl and mix well. Put about half the mixture in the base of the casserole. Top with the pork and add the remaining cabbage mixture. Sprinkle in the lemon juice and add the strip of rind. Cover and cook in the preheated oven for 1$\frac{1}{2}$ hours.

Transfer the pork to a plate. Transfer the cabbage mixture to the plate with a slotted spoon and keep warm. Bring the cooking juices to the boil and reduce slightly. Serve the pork in slices with the cabbage mixture. Spoon over the cooking juices. Garnish with lemon wedges.

SERVES 4

1 tbsp sunflower oil

1 boned and rolled pork loin joint, weighing 750 g/1 lb 10 oz

1 onion, finely chopped

500 g/1 lb 2 oz red cabbage, thick stems discarded and leaves shredded

2 large Bramley apples, peeled, cored and sliced

3 cloves

1 tsp soft light brown sugar

3 tbsp lemon juice

thinly pared strip of lemon rind

lemon wedges, to garnish

SLOW-ROASTED PORK

Preheat the oven to 150°C/300°F/ Gas Mark 2.

Using a small, sharp knife, cut slits all over the pork, opening them out slightly to make little pockets.

Put the garlic slices in a small sieve and rinse under cold running water to moisten. Spread the fennel out on a saucer and roll the garlic slices in it to coat.

Slide the garlic slices and the cloves into the pockets in the pork. Season the meat all over with salt and pepper.

Put the pork in a large ovenproof dish or roasting tin. Pour in the white wine and water. Roast in the preheated oven, basting occasionally, for $2^1/_2$–$2^3/_4$ hours, until the pork is tender but still quite moist.

If you are serving the pork hot, transfer it to a carving board and cut into slices. If you are serving it cold, leave it to cool completely in the cooking juices before removing and slicing.

SERVES 6

1 boned and rolled pork loin joint, weighing 1.6 kg/3 lb 8 oz

4 garlic cloves, thinly sliced lengthways

$1^1/_2$ tsp finely chopped fresh fennel fronds or $^1/_2$ tsp dried fennel

4 cloves

300 ml/10 fl oz dry white wine

300 ml/10 fl oz water

salt and pepper

ROAST VENISON WITH BRANDY SAUCE

Preheat the oven to 180°C/350°F/ Gas Mark 4.

Heat half the oil in a frying pan over a high heat. Season the venison to taste with salt and pepper, add to the pan and cook until lightly browned all over. Pour the remaining oil into a roasting tin. Add the venison, cover with foil and roast in the preheated oven, basting occasionally, for 1¹/₂ hours, or until cooked through. Remove from the oven and transfer to a warmed serving platter. Cover loosely with foil and leave to rest.

To make the sauce, stir the flour into the roasting tin over a medium heat and cook, stirring constantly, for 1 minute. Stir in the stock, scraping the sediment from the base of the tin. Gradually stir in the brandy and bring to the boil, then reduce the heat and simmer, stirring frequently, for 10 minutes, or until the sauce has thickened a little. Remove from the heat and stir in the cream.

Garnish the venison with thyme sprigs and serve with the brandy sauce and a selection of vegetables.

SERVES 4

6 tbsp vegetable oil

1 saddle of fresh venison, weighing 1.7 kg/3 lb 12 oz, trimmed

salt and pepper

fresh thyme sprigs, to garnish

selection of vegetables, to serve

BRANDY SAUCE

1 tbsp plain flour

4 tbsp vegetable stock

175 ml/6 fl oz brandy

100 ml/3¹/₂ fl oz double cream

BOTH WILD AND FARMED VENISON IS SURPRISINGLY INEXPENSIVE COMPARED WITH LAMB OR BEEF. IT MAY BE FRESH OR FROZEN. VENISON HAS A DELICATE TEXTURE AND IS HIGH IN PROTEIN, BUT LOW IN FAT, SO IT IS VERY NUTRITIOUS.

ROAST LAMB WITH GARLIC AND ROSEMARY

SERVES 6

1 leg of lamb, weighing 1.5 kg/
3 lb 5 oz

6 garlic cloves, thinly sliced
lengthways

8 fresh rosemary sprigs

4 tbsp olive oil

salt and pepper

GLAZE

4 tbsp redcurrant jelly

300 ml/10 fl oz rosé wine

Preheat the oven to 200°C/400°F/
Gas Mark 6. Using a small, sharp
knife, cut slits all over the leg of
lamb. Insert 1–2 garlic slices and
4–5 rosemary needles into each slit.
Put any remaining rosemary in the
base of a roasting tin. Season the
lamb to taste with salt and pepper
and put in the roasting tin. Pour
over the oil. Cover with foil and
roast in the preheated oven for
1 hour 20 minutes.

Mix the redcurrant jelly and wine
together in a small saucepan. Heat
over a low heat, stirring constantly,
until combined. Bring to the boil,
then reduce the heat and simmer
until reduced. Remove the lamb
from the oven and pour over the
glaze. Return to the oven and roast,
uncovered, for about 10 minutes,
depending on how well done you
like it.

Remove the lamb from the
roasting tin and transfer to a
carving board. Cover loosely with
foil and leave to rest for 15 minutes
before carving and serving.

ROAST LAMB WITH ORZO

Preheat the oven to 180°C/350°F/ Gas Mark 4.

Untie the lamb and open out. Arrange the lemon slices down the centre and sprinkle over half the oregano, the chopped garlic and salt and pepper to taste. Roll up the meat and tie with string. Cut slits all over the lamb and insert a garlic slice into each slit.

Put the tomatoes with their juice, cold water, remaining oregano, the sugar and bay leaf in a large roasting tin. Put the lamb on top, drizzle over the oil and season to taste with salt and pepper.

Roast the lamb in the preheated oven for 1 hour 5 minutes. Fifteen minutes before the end of the cooking time, stir the boiling water and orzo into the tomatoes in the tin. Add a little extra water if the sauce seems too thick. Return to the oven for a further 15 minutes, or until the lamb and orzo are tender and the tomatoes are reduced to a thick sauce.

To serve, carve the lamb into slices and serve hot with the orzo and tomato sauce.

SERVES 4

1 boned leg or shoulder of lamb, weighing 750 g/ 1 lb 10 oz

$^{1}/_{2}$ lemon, thinly sliced

1 tbsp chopped fresh oregano

4 large garlic cloves, 2 finely chopped and 2 thinly sliced

800 g/1 lb 12 oz canned chopped tomatoes in juice

150 ml/5 fl oz cold water

pinch of sugar

1 bay leaf

2 tbsp olive oil

150 ml/5 fl oz boiling water

225 g/8 oz orzo or short-grain rice

salt and pepper

ORZO IS A VERY SMALL FORM OF PASTA THAT LOOKS LIKE FLAT WHEAT GRAINS. IT IS USED IN SOUP AND MEAT DISHES AND SERVED AS AN ACCOMPANIMENT. IN THIS RECIPE IT IS BAKED WITH LAMB AND ABSORBS THE MEAT JUICES, GIVING IT THE MOST WONDERFUL FLAVOUR.

POT ROASTED LEG OF LAMB

SERVES 4

1 leg of lamb, weighing
1.6 kg/3 lb 8 oz

3–4 fresh rosemary sprigs

115 g/4 oz streaky
bacon rashers

4 tbsp olive oil

2–3 garlic cloves, crushed

2 onions, sliced

2 carrots, sliced

2 celery sticks, sliced

300 ml/10 fl oz dry white wine

1 tbsp tomato purée

300 ml/10 fl oz lamb or
chicken stock

3 medium tomatoes, peeled,
quartered and deseeded

1 tbsp chopped fresh parsley

1 tbsp chopped fresh oregano
or marjoram

salt and pepper

fresh rosemary sprigs,
to garnish

Preheat the oven to 160°C/325°F/ Gas Mark 3.

Wipe the lamb all over with kitchen paper, trim off any excess fat and season to taste with salt and pepper, rubbing well in. Lay the rosemary over the lamb, cover evenly with the bacon rashers and tie in place with kitchen string.

Heat the oil in a frying pan and fry the lamb over a medium heat for 10 minutes, turning several times. Remove from the pan.

Transfer the oil to a large flameproof casserole and cook the garlic and onions for 3–4 minutes until the onions are beginning to soften. Add the carrots and celery and cook for a further few minutes.

Lay the lamb on top of the vegetables and press down to partly submerge. Pour the wine over the lamb, add the tomato purée and simmer for 3–4 minutes. Add the stock, tomatoes and herbs and season to taste with salt and pepper. Return to the boil for 3–4 minutes. Cover the casserole tightly and cook in the oven for 2–2½ hours until very tender.

Remove the lamb from the casserole and remove the bacon and herbs together with the string. Keep the lamb warm. Strain the juices, skimming off any excess fat, and serve in a jug. The vegetables may be put around the joint or in a dish. Garnish with sprigs of rosemary.

BEEF POT ROAST WITH POTATOES AND DILL

SERVES 6

2$\frac{1}{2}$ tbsp plain flour

1 tsp salt

$\frac{1}{4}$ tsp pepper

1 rolled brisket joint, weighing 1.6 kg/3 lb 8 oz

2 tbsp vegetable oil

2 tbsp butter

1 onion, finely chopped

2 celery sticks, diced

2 carrots, diced

1 tsp dill seed

1 tsp dried thyme or oregano

350 ml/12 fl oz full-bodied red wine

150–225 ml/5–8 fl oz beef stock

4–5 potatoes, cut into large chunks and boiled until just tender

2 tbsp chopped fresh dill, to garnish

Preheat the oven to 140°C/275°F/ Gas Mark 1.

Mix 2 tablespoons of the flour with the salt and pepper in a shallow dish. Dip the meat into the mixture to coat. Heat the oil in a flameproof casserole. Add the brisket and cook until browned all over. Transfer to a plate.

Melt half the butter in the casserole over a medium heat. Add the onion, celery, carrots, dill seed and thyme and cook, stirring frequently, for 5 minutes. Return the meat and juices to the casserole.

Pour in the wine and enough stock to reach one-third of the way up the meat. Bring to the boil, then reduce the heat, cover and cook in the preheated oven for 3 hours, turning the meat every 30 minutes. After the meat has been cooking for 2 hours, add the potatoes and more stock, if necessary.

When ready, transfer the meat and vegetables to a warmed serving dish. Sieve the cooking liquid into a saucepan.

Mix the remaining butter and flour to a paste. Bring the cooking liquid to the boil. Whisk in small pieces of the flour and butter paste, whisking constantly until the sauce is smooth. Pour the sauce over the meat and vegetables. Sprinkle with the fresh dill and serve immediately.

ROAST BEEF

SERVES 8

1 prime rib of beef, weighing
2.7 kg/6 lb

2 tsp English mustard powder

3 tbsp plain flour

300 ml/10 fl oz full-bodied
red wine

300 ml/10 fl oz beef stock

2 tsp Worcestershire sauce
(optional)

salt and pepper

Preheat the oven to 230°C/450°F/
Gas Mark 8.

Season the meat to taste with salt
and pepper and rub in the mustard
and 1 tablespoon of the flour.

Put the meat in a roasting tin
large enough to hold it comfortably
and roast in the preheated oven for
15 minutes. Reduce the heat to
190°C/375°F/Gas Mark 5 and cook
for 1 hour 45 minutes for rare beef
or 2 hours 20 minutes for medium
beef. Baste the meat occasionally to
keep it moist. If the tin becomes too
dry, add a little stock or red wine.

When the meat is cooked, transfer
to a warmed serving plate, cover
loosely with foil and leave to rest for
10–15 minutes.

To make the gravy, pour off most
of the fat from the roasting tin, then
put the tin over a medium heat and
scrape the sediment from the base.
Sprinkle in the remaining flour and
quickly whisk it into the juices. When
you have a smooth paste, gradually
add the wine and most of the stock,
whisking constantly. Bring to the
boil, then reduce the heat and cook
for 2–3 minutes until thickened.
Season to taste with salt and pepper,
add the remaining stock, if necessary,
and add a little Worcestershire
sauce, if you like.

When ready to serve, carve the
meat into slices and serve on
warmed plates. Pour the gravy into
a warmed jug to serve.

6

CASSEROLES
AND STEWS

Meat's versatility and diversity really comes into its own when it comes to casseroles and stews. In this chapter you'll find a whole range of eating experiences, from the spicy to the smooth, with numerous delicious stops along the way. There are many international favourites here, such as Lamb Tagine, Milanese Veal, Lone Star Chilli and Beef Bourguignon, or you might like to try something new, such as Rabbit with Prunes or Beef Stew with Olives.

CHICKEN, SAUSAGE AND BEAN STEW

Heat the oil in a large, heavy-based saucepan over a medium–high heat. Add the chicken, pork sausage and frankfurters and cook until lightly browned all over. Reduce the heat to medium. Add the onion and carrots and cook, stirring frequently, for 5 minutes, or until softened.

Stir in the garlic, thyme and chilli flakes and cook, stirring, for 1 minute. Stir in the tomatoes with their juice, beans and stock. Season to taste with salt and pepper. Bring to the boil, then reduce the heat and simmer over a low heat, stirring occasionally, for 20–30 minutes.

Garnish with chopped parsley just before serving.

SERVES 4

2 tbsp vegetable oil

4 boneless, skinless chicken breasts, about 115 g/4 oz each, cubed

225 g/8 oz coarse-textured pork sausage, cut into large chunks

4 frankfurter sausages, halved

1 onion, finely chopped

3 carrots, thinly sliced

1 garlic clove, very finely chopped

1 tsp dried thyme

$^1/_4$–$^1/_2$ tsp dried chilli flakes

400 g/14 oz canned chopped tomatoes in juice

400 g/14 oz canned cannellini beans, drained and rinsed

150 ml/5 fl oz chicken stock

salt and pepper

chopped fresh flat-leaf parsley, to garnish

CHICKEN, BEANS AND SPINACH WITH OLIVES

Heat the oil in a casserole over a medium–high heat. Add the chicken and cook until lightly browned all over. Reduce the heat to medium. Add the onion and celery and cook, stirring frequently, for 5 minutes, or until softened.

Stir in the garlic, rosemary and chilli flakes and cook, stirring, for 1 minute. Stir in the tomatoes with their juice, beans and stock. Season to taste with salt and pepper.

Bring to the boil, then reduce the heat and simmer over a medium–low heat, stirring occasionally, for 20 minutes. Stir in the spinach leaves and cook for 3 minutes, or until just wilted.

Garnish with the sliced olives and serve immediately.

SERVES 4

2 tbsp olive oil

600 g/1 lb 5 oz skinless, boneless chicken breasts, cut into chunks

1 small onion, finely chopped

2 celery sticks, diced

3 large garlic cloves, finely chopped

2 tsp chopped fresh rosemary

1/4 tsp dried chilli flakes

400 g/14 oz canned chopped tomatoes in juice

400 g/14 oz canned cannellini beans, drained and rinsed

250 ml/9 fl oz chicken stock

350 g/12 oz baby spinach leaves, roughly chopped

salt and pepper

8–10 stoned black olives, sliced, to garnish

HUNTER'S CHICKEN

Preheat the oven to 160°C/325°F/ Gas Mark 3. Melt the butter with the oil in a flameproof casserole. Add the chicken pieces and cook until lightly browned all over. Using a slotted spoon, transfer to a plate.

Add the onions and garlic to the casserole and cook over a low heat, stirring occasionally, for 10 minutes until golden. Add the tomatoes with their juice, the parsley, basil, tomato purée and wine and season to taste with salt and pepper. Bring to the boil, then return the chicken pieces to the casserole, pushing them down into the sauce.

Cover the casserole, transfer to the preheated oven and cook for 50 minutes. Add the mushrooms and cook for a further 10 minutes, or until the chicken is tender and the juices run clear when a skewer is inserted into the thickest part of the meat. Serve immediately.

SERVES 4

15 g/¹/₂ oz unsalted butter

2 tbsp olive oil

1.8 kg/4 lb skinless chicken portions, on the bone

2 red onions, sliced

2 garlic cloves, finely chopped

400 g/14 oz canned chopped tomatoes in juice

2 tbsp chopped fresh flat-leaved parsley

6 fresh basil leaves, torn

1 tbsp sun-dried tomato purée

150 ml/5 fl oz full-bodied red wine

225 g/8 oz mushrooms, sliced

salt and pepper

YOU CAN SUBSTITUTE MARSALA FOR THE RED WINE AND ADD 1 GREEN PEPPER, DESEEDED AND SLICED, WITH THE ONIONS AND GARLIC.

LOMBARDY DUCKLING

SERVES 4

1 duckling, weighing 2.25 kg/
5 lb

225 g/8 oz small brown lentils

1 tbsp virgin olive oil

2 onions

2 celery sticks

2 tbsp brandy or grappa

150 ml/5 fl oz dry white wine

1 tsp cornflour

salt and pepper

STOCK

wings, backbone and neck from
the duckling

1 celery stick

1 garlic clove

6 peppercorns, lightly crushed

1 bay leaf

5 fresh flat-leaf parsley sprigs

1 onion

1 clove

large pinch of salt

Cut the duckling into joints. Cut off the wings. Fold back the skin at the neck end and cut out the wishbone with a small, sharp knife. Using poultry shears or heavy kitchen scissors, cut the breast in half along the breastbone, from the tail end to the neck. Cut along each side of the backbone to separate the 2 halves. Remove the backbone. Cut each portion in half diagonally.

To make the stock, put the wings, backbone and neck, if available, in a large saucepan and add the celery, garlic, peppercorns, bay leaf and parsley. Stick the onion with the clove and add to the saucepan with the salt. Add cold water to cover and bring to the boil. Skim off any scum that rises to the surface, then reduce the heat and simmer very gently for 2 hours. Sieve into a clean saucepan and boil until reduced and concentrated. Reserve the stock, keeping 150 ml/5fl oz separate from the rest.

Rinse and pick over the lentils, then place in a saucepan. Add cold water to cover and add the oil. Cut an onion in half and add with a celery stick. Bring to the boil over medium heat, then reduce the heat and simmer for 15 minutes, or until the lentils are just beginning to soften. Drain and reserve.

Meanwhile, put the duckling pieces, skin-side down, in a heavy-based frying pan and cook, gently shaking the frying pan occasionally, for 10 minutes. Transfer to a flameproof casserole and drain off the excess fat from the frying pan.

Finely chop the remaining onion and celery and add to the frying pan. Cook over a low heat, stirring occasionally, for 5 minutes, until softened. Using a slotted spoon, transfer the vegetables to the casserole.

Set the casserole over a medium heat, add the brandy and ignite. When the flames have died down, add the wine and the reserved measured stock. Bring to the boil, add the lentils and season to taste with pepper. Cover and simmer gently over a low heat for 40 minutes, until the lentils and duck are tender and the juices run clear when a skewer is inserted into the thickest part of the meat.

Blend the cornflour with 2 tablespoons of the remaining reserved stock to a smooth paste in a small bowl. Stir the paste into the casserole and cook, stirring constantly, for 5 minutes, or until thickened. Add salt to taste and adjust the seasoning, if necessary. Serve immediately.

PHEASANT AND CHESTNUT CASSEROLE

Preheat the oven to 180°C/350°F/ Gas Mark 4. Melt the oil with the butter in a large frying pan over a high heat. Add the pheasant joints and cook until browned all over. Using a slotted spoon, transfer the pheasant to a casserole.

Add the bacon to the frying pan and cook over a medium heat, stirring, for 3–4 minutes until crisp and golden. Transfer to the casserole.

Add the chestnuts to the frying pan and cook over a low heat, stirring frequently, for 3–4 minutes until lightly browned, then transfer to the casserole.

Add the onions and garlic to the frying pan and cook over a medium heat, stirring, for 2–3 minutes until the onions are softened.

Stir in the flour and mix well. Gradually add the stock, scraping the sediment from the base of the frying pan, and bring to the boil. Pour in the wine. Pour over the pheasant in the casserole.

Add the orange rind and juice and the redcurrant jelly. Season well, cover and cook in the centre of the preheated oven for 1$\frac{1}{2}$–2 hours until the pheasant is tender. Turn the joints in the sauce halfway through the cooking time.

Remove from the oven, then check the seasoning and adjust, if necessary.

Serve hot, garnished with the orange slices and watercress.

SERVES 4

1 tbsp olive oil

2 tbsp butter

1 large oven-ready pheasant, jointed

175 g/6 oz lardons or streaky bacon, cut into strips

225 g/8 oz vacuum-packed chestnuts

2 onions, thinly sliced

1 garlic clove, chopped

2 tbsp plain flour

425 ml/15 fl oz game or vegetable stock

150 ml/5 fl oz full-bodied red wine

grated rind and juice of 1 orange

2 tbsp redcurrant jelly

salt and pepper

TO GARNISH

1 orange, sliced

small bunch of watercress

VENISON CASSEROLE

SERVES 4–6

3 tbsp olive oil

1 kg/2 lb 4 oz casserole venison, cut into 3-cm/1¼-inch cubes

2 onions, thinly sliced

2 garlic cloves, chopped

2 tbsp plain flour

350 ml/12 fl oz beef or vegetable stock

125 ml/4 fl oz port or red wine

2 tbsp redcurrant jelly

6 juniper berries, crushed

pinch of ground cinnamon

freshly grated nutmeg

175 g/6 oz vacuum-packed chestnuts (optional)

salt and pepper

baked or mashed potatoes, to serve

Preheat the oven to 150°C/300°F/ Gas Mark 2.

Heat the oil in a large frying pan over a high heat. Add the venison, in batches if necessary, and cook until browned all over. Using a slotted spoon, transfer to a large casserole.

Add the onions and garlic to the frying pan and cook over a medium heat, stirring frequently, for 8 minutes, or until golden. Transfer to the casserole. Sprinkle the meat in the casserole with the flour and turn to coat evenly.

Gradually add the stock to the frying pan, stirring well and scraping the sediment from the base of the frying pan, then bring to the boil. Transfer to the casserole and stir well, ensuring that the meat is just covered.

Add the port, redcurrant jelly, juniper berries, cinnamon, a little freshly grated nutmeg and the chestnuts, if using. Season well with salt and pepper and stir well. Cover and cook in the centre of the preheated oven for 2–2½ hours.

Remove from the oven and adjust the seasoning, if necessary. Serve immediately, piping hot, with baked or mashed potatoes.

THIS CASSEROLE BENEFITS FROM BEING MADE THE DAY BEFORE TO ALLOW THE FLAVOURS TO DEVELOP. REHEAT GENTLY BEFORE SERVING. COOL THE CASSEROLE AS QUICKLY AS POSSIBLE AND STORE IN THE REFRIGERATOR OR A COOL LARDER OVERNIGHT.

RABBIT WITH PRUNES

Put the flour with salt and pepper to taste in a polythene bag, add the rabbit pieces and shake well to coat each piece.

Melt the butter with the oil in a large sauté or frying pan with a tight-fitting lid or a flameproof casserole over a medium–high heat. Add the rabbit pieces, in batches if necessary, and cook until lightly browned all over. Using a slotted spoon, transfer to a plate.

Add the shallots, tomato and garlic to the fat remaining in the pan and cook, stirring frequently, for 3 minutes, or until the shallots are softened but not browned. Return the rabbit pieces to the pan. Add the wine and water to just cover the rabbit – the exact amount will depend on the width of the pan.

Stir in the bouquet garni, cloves, peppercorns, ginger, cinnamon and salt and pepper to taste. Bring to the boil, stirring, then reduce the heat to low, cover and simmer for 45 minutes.

Stir in the prunes and raisins, cover and simmer for a further 15 minutes, or until the rabbit pieces are tender when pierced with the tip of a knife. Remove the bouquet garni.

Meanwhile, to make the caramel, put the sugar and water in a small saucepan over a high heat, stirring until the sugar dissolves. Bring to the boil, without stirring, then continue to boil until the syrup turns a dark golden caramel colour. Immediately add the vinegar to prevent further cooking.

Stir the caramel into the sauce in the sauté pan. Transfer the rabbit pieces to a serving platter, cover loosely with foil and keep warm. Bring the sauce to the boil and leave to bubble and reduce for 2–3 minutes until it has a coating consistency. Taste and adjust the seasoning, if necessary.

Serve the rabbit pieces with the sauce and fruit spooned over, garnished with chopped parsley.

TO PEEL THE TOMATO, USE A SHARP KNIFE TO MARK A CROSS ON THE BASE, THEN PLACE IT IN A HEATPROOF BOWL AND COVER WITH BOILING WATER. LEAVE FOR 5 MINUTES, RINSE UNDER COLD WATER AND PEEL OFF THE SKIN. QUARTER, DESEED AND CHOP THE FLESH.

SERVES 4–6

2 tablespoons plain flour

1 rabbit, weighing 1.25 kg/2 lb 12 oz, cut into 8 pieces

25 g/1 oz unsalted butter

1 tbsp sunflower oil

2 shallots, finely chopped

1 large tomato, peeled, deseeded and diced (see below left)

1 large garlic clove, crushed

250 ml/9 fl oz full-bodied red wine

250 ml/9 fl oz water

1 bouquet garni

3 cloves

3 black peppercorns, crushed

1/2 tsp ground ginger

1/4 tsp ground cinnamon

12–16 ready-to-eat prunes

3 tbsp raisins

salt and pepper

chopped fresh flat-leaf parsley, to garnish

CARAMEL

40 g/1 1/2 oz caster sugar

2 tbsp water

1/2 tsp red wine vinegar

PORK HOTPOT

Spread the flour out on a plate and season to taste with salt and pepper. Toss the pork slices in the flour to coat, shaking off any excess. Heat the oil in a flameproof casserole over a medium heat. Add the pork slices and cook until browned all over. Using a slotted spoon, transfer the pork to a plate.

Add the onions to the casserole and cook over a low heat, stirring occasionally, for 10 minutes, or until golden brown. Add the garlic and cook, stirring, for 2 minutes, then add the tomatoes with their juice, the wine and basil leaves and season

to taste with salt and pepper. Cook, stirring frequently, for 3 minutes.

Return the pork to the casserole, cover and simmer gently for 1 hour, or until the meat is tender. Stir in the chopped parsley.

Serve immediately, garnished with parsley sprigs and accompanied by fresh crusty bread.

SERVES 6

85 g/3 oz plain flour

1.3 kg/3 lb pork fillet, cut into 5-mm/¼-inch slices

4 tbsp sunflower oil

2 onions, thinly sliced

2 garlic cloves, finely chopped

400 g/14 oz canned chopped tomatoes in juice

350 ml/12 fl oz dry white wine

1 tbsp torn fresh basil leaves

2 tbsp chopped fresh parsley, plus extra sprigs to garnish

salt and pepper

fresh crusty bread, to serve

BRAISED PORK WITH GARLIC AND HERBS

Preheat the oven to 160°C/325°F/ Gas Mark 3. Put the pork, garlic, herbs, peppercorns, pinch of salt and water to cover in a flameproof casserole. Cover and bring to the boil, skimming occasionally to remove any scum that rises to the surface. Transfer to the preheated oven and cook, turning the pork occasionally, for 3 hours, or until very tender.

Remove the pork. Sieve the stock into a large jug. Rinse the casserole, add a ladleful of the stock and bring to the boil. Add the pork and cook over a medium heat until the liquid has almost evaporated. Continue adding the stock, a ladleful at a time, turning the pork occasionally, until 2 ladlefuls remain.

Transfer the pork to a carving board, cover loosely with foil and leave to rest. Add the wine to the casserole, bring to the boil and cook for 1 minute. Add the remaining stock and boil until reduced by half. Whisk in the butter, a little at a time, then season to taste with salt and pepper.

Carve the pork into thick slices and serve with the sauce, accompanied by green vegetables.

SERVES 6

1 boned and rolled leg of pork, weighing 1.5 kg/3 lb 5 oz

12 garlic cloves, peeled

2 fresh rosemary sprigs

2 fresh sage leaves

4 black peppercorns, lightly crushed

125 ml/4 fl oz dry white wine

25 g/1 oz butter, diced

salt and pepper

green vegetables, to serve

SAUSAGES WITH BORLOTTI BEANS

SERVES 4

2 tbsp virgin olive oil

500 g/1 lb 2 oz sausages

140 g/5 oz smoked pancetta or streaky bacon, diced

2 red onions, chopped

2 garlic cloves, finely chopped

225 g/8 oz dried borlotti beans, soaked overnight in cold water

2 tsp finely chopped fresh rosemary, plus extra sprigs to garnish

2 tsp chopped fresh sage

300 ml/10 fl oz dry white wine

300 ml/10 fl oz water

salt and pepper

fresh crusty bread, to serve

Preheat the oven to 140°C/275°F/ Gas Mark 1. Heat the oil in a flameproof casserole over a low heat. Add the sausages and cook until browned all over. Using a slotted spoon, transfer to a plate.

Add the pancetta to the casserole, increase the heat to medium and cook, stirring frequently, for 5 minutes, or until golden brown. Using a slotted spoon, transfer to the plate.

Add the onions to the casserole and cook over a low heat, stirring occasionally, for 5 minutes, or until softened. Add the garlic and cook, stirring, for 2 minutes.

Drain the beans and rinse under cold running water. Put in a large saucepan of cold water, bring to the boil and skim off the scum that rises to the surface. Boil rapidly for 10 minutes, then drain.

Add the beans to the casserole, then return the sausages and pancetta. Gently stir in the herbs and pour in the wine and water. Season to taste with pepper. Slowly bring to the boil and boil for 15 minutes, then cover, transfer to the preheated oven and cook for $2^{3}/_{4}$ hours. Taste and add salt if necessary.

To serve, ladle the sausages and beans onto 4 warmed serving plates. Garnish with rosemary sprigs and serve immediately with fresh crusty bread.

THE BITTER-SWEET FLAVOUR OF BORLOTTI BEANS MAKES A PERFECT CONTRAST TO THE SPICINESS OF THE SAUSAGES AND THE SMOKY PANCETTA, BUT OTHER BEANS, SUCH AS CANNELLINI, WOULD WORK WELL TOO.

MARINATED PORK WITH GARLIC

SERVES 6

5 tbsp rice vinegar

4 tbsp dark soy sauce

1 tbsp coriander seeds, crushed

1 kg/2 lb 4 oz boneless pork, cut into 2.5–4-cm/1–1¹/₂-inch cubes

1 garlic bulb, separated into cloves and peeled

2 tbsp groundnut or sunflower oil

350 g/12 oz sweet potatoes, peeled and cubed

8 black peppercorns, lightly crushed

Mix the vinegar, soy sauce and crushed coriander seeds together in a shallow, non-metallic dish. Add the pork cubes and turn to coat in the marinade. Cover and leave to marinate in the refrigerator for 1 hour.

Slice the garlic cloves lengthways. Remove the pork from the marinade, reserving the marinade. Heat the oil in a heavy-based saucepan over a high heat. Add the garlic and cook, stirring, for 1 minute. Reduce the heat to medium, add the pork and cook,

stirring, for 5 minutes. Add the sweet potatoes, peppercorns, the reserved marinade and water to cover. Bring to the boil, skim off any scum that rises to the surface, then reduce the heat, cover and simmer for 30 minutes.

Uncover the pan, increase the heat to high and cook, stirring frequently, for 25 minutes, or until the pork is tender and the sauce is slightly thickened. Serve hot.

LAMB TAGINE

SERVES 4

1 tbsp sunflower or corn oil

1 onion, chopped

350 g/12 oz boneless lamb, trimmed of all visible fat and cut into 2.5-cm/1-inch cubes

1 garlic clove, finely chopped

600 ml/1 pint vegetable stock

grated rind and juice of 1 orange

1 tsp clear honey

1 cinnamon stick

1-cm/$\frac{1}{2}$-inch piece fresh root ginger, finely chopped

1 aubergine

4 tomatoes, peeled and chopped

115 g/4 oz ready-to-eat dried apricots

2 tbsp chopped fresh coriander

salt and pepper

couscous, to serve

Heat the oil in a large, heavy-based frying pan with a tight-fitting lid or flameproof casserole over a medium heat. Add the onion and lamb cubes and cook until the meat is lightly browned all over. Add the garlic, stock, orange rind and juice, honey, cinnamon stick and ginger. Bring to the boil, then reduce the heat, cover and simmer for 45 minutes.

Halve the aubergine lengthways and thinly slice. Add to the frying pan with the tomatoes and apricots. Cover and cook for a further 45 minutes, until the lamb is tender.

Stir in the coriander, season to taste with salt and pepper and serve immediately, straight from the frying pan, with couscous.

BRAISED LAMB SHANKS WITH CANNELLINI BEANS

Preheat the oven to 160°C/325°F/ Gas Mark 3. Drain the beans and rinse under cold running water. Put in a large saucepan of cold water, bring to the boil and skim off the scum that rises to the surface. Boil rapidly for 10 minutes, then drain and reserve.

Meanwhile, heat the oil in a large, flameproof casserole over a medium heat. Add the onion and cook, stirring frequently, for 5 minutes, or until softened. Add the carrots and celery and cook, stirring frequently, for 5 minutes, or until beginning to soften and the onion is beginning to brown. Add the garlic and cook, stirring, for 1 minute. Push the vegetables to one side.

Add the lamb shanks to the casserole and cook until browned all over. Add the reserved beans, tomatoes with their juice, the wine and orange rind and juice and stir together. Add the bay leaves and rosemary. Pour in the water so that the liquid comes halfway up the shanks. Season with pepper, but do not add salt as this will prevent the beans softening.

Bring to the boil, then cover, transfer to the preheated oven and cook for 1 hour. Turn the shanks over in the stock and cook for a further 1$\frac{1}{2}$ hours until the lamb and beans are tender. Remove the bay leaves, then taste and add salt and pepper, if necessary. Serve hot.

SERVES 4

250 g/9 oz dried cannellini beans, soaked overnight in cold water

2 tbsp sunflower or corn oil

1 large onion, thinly sliced

4 carrots, chopped

2 celery sticks, thinly sliced

1 garlic clove, chopped

4 large lamb shanks

400 g/14 oz canned chopped tomatoes in juice

300 ml/10 fl oz full-bodied red wine

thinly pared rind and juice of 1 orange

2 bay leaves

3 fresh rosemary sprigs

about 200 ml/7 fl oz water

salt and pepper

MILANESE VEAL

Melt the butter with the oil in a large, heavy-based frying pan over a low heat. Add the onions and leek and cook, stirring occasionally, for 5 minutes, or until softened.

Spread the flour out on a plate and season to taste with salt and pepper. Toss the pieces of veal in the flour to coat, shaking off any excess. Add the veal to the frying pan, increase the heat to high and cook until browned all over.

Gradually stir in the wine and stock and bring just to the boil,

stirring constantly. Reduce the heat, cover and simmer for 1$\frac{1}{4}$ hours, or until the veal is very tender.

Meanwhile, to make the gremolata, mix all the ingredients together in a small bowl.

Using a slotted spoon, transfer the veal to a warmed serving dish and keep warm. Bring the sauce to the boil and cook, stirring occasionally, until thickened and reduced.

Pour the sauce over the veal, sprinkle with the gremolata and serve immediately.

SERVES 4

4 tbsp butter

1 tbsp virgin olive oil

2 onions, chopped

1 leek, chopped

3 tbsp plain flour

4 thick slices veal shin

300 ml/10 fl oz dry white wine

300 ml/10 fl oz veal or chicken stock

GREMOLATA

2 tbsp chopped fresh parsley

1 garlic clove, finely chopped

grated rind of 1 lemon

MODERN VERSIONS OF THIS DISH OFTEN INCLUDE TOMATOES. IF YOU LIKE, ADD 400 G/14 OZ CANNED TOMATOES WITH THE WINE AND STOCK. YOU COULD ALSO ADD 1 FINELY CHOPPED CARROT AND 1 FINELY CHOPPED CELERY STICK WITH THE ONIONS AND LEEK.

BEEF BOURGUIGNON

Preheat the oven to 150°C/300°F/ Gas Mark 2. Melt 25 g/1 oz of the butter with 1 tablespoon of the oil in a large, flameproof casserole over a medium–high heat. Add the lardons and cook for 2 minutes, or until beginning to brown. Remove with a slotted spoon and drain on kitchen paper.

Add the beef, in batches if necessary, and cook until browned all over. Add extra butter or oil as necessary. Transfer to a plate.

Pour off all but 2 tablespoons of the fat from the casserole. Add the garlic, carrot, leek and onion and cook, stirring frequently, for 3 minutes, or until the onion is beginning to soften. Sprinkle in the flour with salt and pepper to taste and cook, stirring, for 2 minutes.

Stir in the wine, stock, tomato purée and the bouquet garni and bring to the boil, scraping the sediment from the base of the casserole. Return the beef and lardons to the casserole and pour in extra stock so that the ingredients are covered by about 1 cm/¹/₂ inch.

Slowly return the casserole to the boil, then cover, transfer to the preheated oven and cook for 2 hours.

Meanwhile, melt 25 g/1 oz of the remaining butter with the remaining oil in a large sauté or frying pan over a medium–high heat. Add the pickling onions and cook, stirring frequently, until golden all over. Remove with a slotted spoon and set aside.

Melt the remaining butter in the sauté pan. Add the mushrooms, season to taste with salt and pepper and cook, stirring, until golden. Remove with a slotted spoon and set aside.

After the casserole has cooked for 2 hours, stir in the pickling onions and mushrooms. Cook for a further 30 minutes, or until the beef is very tender.

Remove the bouquet garni. Taste and adjust the seasoning, if necessary. Sprinkle over the parsley to garnish and serve hot with French bread.

SERVES 4–6

85 g/3 oz butter

2 tbsp sunflower oil

175 g/6 oz smoked lardons, blanched for 30 seconds, drained and patted dry

900 g/2 lb stewing beef, such as chuck or leg, trimmed and cut into 5-cm/2-inch chunks

2 large garlic cloves, crushed

1 carrot, peeled and diced

1 leek, halved and sliced

1 onion, finely chopped

2 tbsp plain flour

350 ml/12 fl oz full-bodied red Burgundy wine

about 500 ml/18 fl oz beef stock

1 tbsp tomato purée

1 bouquet garni

12 pickling onions

12 button mushrooms

salt and pepper

chopped fresh flat-leaf parsley, to garnish

French bread, to serve

LONE STAR CHILLI

Dry-fry the cumin seeds in a heavy-based frying pan over a medium heat, shaking the pan frequently, for 3–4 minutes until lightly toasted. Leave to cool, then crush in a mortar with a pestle. Alternatively, use a coffee grinder.

Put the seasoned flour in a bowl. Toss the beef in the flour to coat, shaking off any excess. Melt the dripping in a large, heavy-based saucepan. Add the beef, in batches, and cook until browned all over. Using a slotted spoon, transfer the beef to a plate.

Add the onions and garlic to the saucepan and cook over a medium heat, stirring, for 5 minutes, or until the onions are softened. Add the cumin, oregano, paprika and chillies and cook, stirring, for 2 minutes. Return the beef to the saucepan, pour over the lager, then add the chocolate. Bring to the boil, stirring, then reduce the heat, cover and leave to simmer for 2–3 hours until the beef is very tender, adding more lager if necessary. Serve with warmed flour tortillas and some soured cream.

SERVES 4

1 tbsp cumin seeds

plain flour, well seasoned with salt and pepper, for coating

650 g/1 lb 7 oz rump steak, cut into 2.5-cm/1-inch cubes

3 tbsp beef dripping, bacon fat or vegetable oil

2 onions, finely chopped

4 garlic cloves, finely chopped

1 tbsp dried oregano

2 tsp paprika

4 dried red chillies, crushed, or to taste

1 large bottle of Spanish lager

115 g/4 oz plain chocolate

TO SERVE

warmed flour tortillas

soured cream

BEEF STEW WITH GARLIC AND SHALLOTS

Spread the flour out on a plate and season to taste with salt and pepper. Toss the steak in the flour to coat. Heat 3 tablespoons of the oil in a large, flameproof casserole. Add the steak, in batches, and cook until browned all over. Using a slotted spoon, transfer to a plate.

Heat the remaining oil in the casserole over medium heat. Add the garlic and cook, stirring frequently, until golden. Add the vinegar and heat until evaporated. Transfer the garlic to the plate.

Melt the butter in the casserole over a low heat. Add the shallots and cook, stirring frequently, for 15 minutes. Remove and set aside.

Return the steak and garlic to the casserole. Add the wine and salt and pepper to taste. Bring to the boil, stirring. Reduce the heat, cover and simmer, stirring occasionally, for 1–1$\frac{1}{4}$ hours. Return the shallots to the casserole, cover and cook for a further 45 minutes, or until the steak is tender. Garnish with thyme sprigs and serve.

SERVES 6

4 tbsp plain flour

1.3 kg/3 lb braising steak, cut into 5-cm/2-inch cubes

4 tbsp sunflower oil

12 garlic cloves, lightly crushed

3 tbsp sherry vinegar

55 g/2 oz butter

850 g/1 lb 14 oz shallots

350 ml/12 fl oz full-bodied red wine

salt and pepper

few fresh thyme sprigs, to garnish

BEEF STEW WITH OLIVES

SERVES 4–6

900 g/2 lb stewing beef, such as chuck or leg, trimmed and cut into 5-cm/2-inch cubes

2 onions, thinly sliced

2 carrots, thickly sliced

4 large garlic cloves, bruised

1 large bouquet garni of 2 fresh flat-leaf parsley sprigs, 2 fresh thyme sprigs and 2 bay leaves, tied to a piece of celery

4 juniper berries

500 ml/18 fl oz full-bodied red wine

2 tbsp brandy

2 tbsp olive oil

225 g/8 oz boned belly of pork, rind removed

200 g/7 oz plain flour

2 x 10-cm/4-inch strips of orange rind

85 g/3 oz black olives, stoned and rinsed

beef stock, if necessary

90 ml/3 fl oz water

salt and pepper

pasta, to serve

TO GARNISH

chopped fresh flat-leaf parsley

finely grated orange rind

Put the beef in a large glass or earthenware bowl and add the onions, carrots, garlic, bouquet garni, juniper berries and salt and pepper to taste. Pour over the wine, brandy and oil and stir well. Cover and leave to marinate in the refrigerator for 24 hours.

Remove the beef and marinade from the refrigerator 30 minutes before cooking. Preheat the oven to 160°C/325°F/Gas Mark 3. Cut the belly of pork into 5-mm/^{1}/$_4$-inch strips. Bring a saucepan of water to the boil and add the pork. Return to the boil and blanch for 3 minutes, then drain.

Remove the beef from the marinade, reserving the marinade, and pat dry with kitchen paper. Put 3 tablespoons of the flour with salt and pepper to taste in a polythene bag, add the beef and shake well to coat each piece.

Transfer half the pork strips to a 3.4-litre/6-pint flameproof casserole. Top with the beef and marinade, including the vegetables and bouquet garni, and add the orange rind and olives. Scatter the remaining pork strips over. If the wine doesn't cover all the ingredients, top up with stock.

Mix the remaining flour with the water in a small bowl to form a thick, pliable paste. Slowly bring the casserole to the boil, then add the lid and use your fingers to press the paste around the rim to form a tight seal. Transfer the casserole to the preheated oven and cook for 1 hour. Reduce the temperature to 140°C/275°F/Gas Mark 1 and cook for a further 3 hours.

Remove the casserole from the oven and use a serrated knife to cut off the seal. Use the tip of the knife to ensure that the beef and carrots are tender. If not, cook for a further 15 minutes.

Using a large metal spoon, skim any fat from the surface. Season to taste. Remove the bouquet garni, garnish with parsley and orange rind and serve with pasta. Alternatively, leave to cool completely, cover and chill overnight. Before reheating, scrape the solid fat off the surface.

7

PIES AND PASTRIES

If you're looking for an alternative to sandwiches, check out the following pages for fresh ideas. Portable picnic food abounds in this chapter, with recipes for tartlets of numerous varieties, from Balsamic Duck and Radicchio to Artichoke and Pancetta. Find out how to make a delicious Raised Pork and Apple Pie or Rosemary Lamb in Filo Pastry. There are numerous supper standbys as well, from traditional Shepherd's Pie to Beef Wellington and Steak and Mushroom Pie.

BALSAMIC DUCK AND RADICCHIO TARTLETS

Grease a 7.5-cm/3-inch, 12-hole muffin tin. To make the pastry, sift the flour and salt into a food processor, add the butter and process until the mixture resembles fine breadcrumbs. Tip into a large bowl. Alternatively, sift the flour and salt into a bowl and rub in the butter with your fingertips until the mixture resembles fine breadcrumbs. Stir in the sugar and mix in a little iced water, just enough to bring the dough together.

Turn out onto a lightly floured work surface and cut the dough in half. Roll out one half and, using a 9-cm/3^1/$_2$-inch pastry cutter, cut out 6 rounds. Roll out each round to 12 cm/4^1/$_2$ inches in diameter and use to line the muffin holes, pressing to fit. Repeat with the remaining dough. Put a piece of baking paper in each hole and fill with baking beans. Chill for 30 minutes. Meanwhile, preheat the oven to 200°C/400°F/Gas Mark 6.

Bake the tartlet cases in the preheated oven for 10 minutes, then remove the paper and beans and bake for a further 5 minutes. Leave to cool in the tin until cold. Leave the oven on.

To make the filling, wipe the duck breasts with kitchen paper, make a series of thin, diagonal cuts in the skin and rub in the salt. Put the duck on a rack set over a roasting tin. Roast for 25–30 minutes until crisp. Meanwhile, melt the butter with the oil in a frying pan over a low heat. Add the onions and sugar and cook, stirring occasionally, for 20–25 minutes, until soft and slightly caramelized. Add the vinegar, radicchio and salt and pepper to taste and cook, stirring frequently, for a further 5 minutes. Remove the duck from the oven and leave to rest for 5 minutes.

Put the tartlet cases on a serving dish and spoon in the onion and radicchio mixture. Slice the duck very thinly and divide between the tarts. Sprinkle with parsley and drizzle with a little more balsamic vinegar. Serve warm.

MAKES 12

PASTRY

100 g/3^1/$_2$ oz butter, diced and chilled, plus extra for greasing

225 g/8 oz plain flour, plus extra for dusting

pinch of salt

^{1}/$_2$ tsp icing sugar

1–2 tbsp iced water

FILLING

2 Gressingham duck breasts, about 175 g/6 oz each

pinch of salt

25g/1 oz butter

1 tbsp olive oil

2 onions, thinly sliced

2 tsp soft light brown sugar

1 tbsp balsamic vinegar, plus extra for drizzling

^{1}/$_2$ large or 1 small radicchio, thinly shredded

salt and pepper

chopped fresh flat-leaf parsley, to garnish

READY-COOKED CHINESE DUCK WOULD ALSO WORK WELL IF REHEATED AND SHREDDED. SUBSTITUTE SOY SAUCE FOR THE BALSAMIC VINEGAR AND SIMMER UNTIL THICK, THEN DRIZZLE OVER THE DUCK AND TOP WITH SHREDDED SPRING ONION. THINLY PARED STRIPS OF ORANGE RIND WOULD ALSO MAKE AN ATTRACTIVE GARNISH.

QUICHE LORRAINE TARTLETS

MAKES 6

PASTRY

175 g/6 oz plain flour

pinch of salt

75 g/3 oz chilled unsalted butter, diced

2–3 tbsp iced water

FILLING

125 g/4½ oz unsmoked lardons

2 large eggs

225 ml/8 fl oz whipping cream

125 g/4½ oz Gruyère cheese, grated

freshly grated nutmeg

salt and pepper

Grease 6 x 12-cm/4½-inch tart tins. To make the pastry, sift the flour and salt into a food processor, add the butter and process until the mixture resembles fine breadcrumbs. Alternatively, sift the flour and salt into a bowl and rub in the butter with your fingertips until the mixture resembles fine breadcrumbs. Tip into a large bowl, if necessary, and mix in about 2 tablespoons of iced water, just enough to bring the dough together. Lightly sprinkle with extra water.

Turn out onto a lightly floured work surface and cut into 6 equal-sized pieces. Roll out each piece and use to line each tart tin,

pressing to fit. Leave the excess pastry hanging over the edges of the rims. Put a piece of baking paper into each tartlet and fill with baking beans. Chill for 30 minutes. Meanwhile, preheat the oven to 200°C/400°F/Gas Mark 6.

Bake the tartlet cases in the preheated oven for 5 minutes, or until the rim is set. Remove the paper and beans, then return the tart cases to the oven and bake for a further 5 minutes, or until the bases look dry. Leave the tart cases on the baking tray and remove from the oven. Reduce the oven temperature to 190°C/375°F/Gas Mark 5.

Meanwhile, put the lardons in a sauté or frying pan over a low heat and sauté for 3 minutes, or until the fat begins to melt. Increase the heat to medium and continue sautéeing until they are crisp.

Sprinkle the lardons over the pastry case. Beat the eggs, cream and cheese together, then season to taste with the salt and pepper and nutmeg. Carefully divide the filling between the pastry cases, then transfer the tarts to the oven to bake for 20–25 minutes until the filling is set and the pastry is golden brown. Transfer the quiches to a wire rack to cool completely, then remove from the tins.

PEA, HAM AND CRÈME FRAÎCHE TARTLETS

Grease 6 x 9-cm/3¹/₂-inch loose-based fluted tart tins. To make the pastry, sift the flour and salt into a food processor, add the butter and process until the mixture resembles fine breadcrumbs. Alternatively, sift the flour and salt into a bowl and rub in the butter with your fingertips until the mixture resembles fine breadcrumbs. Tip into a large bowl, if necessary, stir in the Parmesan cheese and mix in a little iced water, just enough to bring the dough together.

Turn out onto a lightly floured work surface and cut into 6 equal-sized pieces. Roll out each piece and use to line each tart tin, pressing to fit. Roll the rolling pin over the tins to neaten the edges and trim the excess pastry. Put a piece of baking paper into each tartlet and fill with baking beans. Chill for 30 minutes. Meanwhile, preheat the oven to 200°C/400°F/Gas Mark 6.

Bake the tartlet cases in the preheated oven for 10 minutes, then remove the paper and beans.

Meanwhile, to make the filling, cook the peas in a saucepan of boiling water for 3–4 minutes until just tender, then drain. Melt the butter in a frying pan over a low heat. Add the shallots and cook, stirring occasionally, for 10 minutes. Add the ham and cook, stirring, for 3–5 minutes. Add the peas and mint, remove from the heat and stir in the crème fraîche and egg yolks. Season to taste with salt and pepper. Divide between the tartlet cases. Bake for 12–15 minutes.

MAKES 6

PASTRY

70 g/2¹/₂ oz butter, diced and chilled, plus extra for greasing

125 g/4¹/₂ oz plain flour, plus extra for dusting

pinch of salt

25 g/1 oz freshly grated Parmesan cheese

1–2 tbsp iced water

FILLING

200 g/7 oz fresh or frozen peas

25 g/1 oz unsalted butter

2 shallots, finely chopped

100 g/3¹/₂ oz cooked ham, chopped

3–4 fresh mint leaves, chopped

125 ml/4 fl oz crème fraîche

3 egg yolks

salt and pepper

ARTICHOKE AND PANCETTA TARTLETS

MAKES 6

PASTRY

70 g/2¹/₂ oz butter, diced and chilled, plus extra for greasing

125 g/4¹/₂ oz plain flour, plus extra for dusting

pinch of salt

1–2 tbsp iced water

FILLING

5 tbsp double cream

4 tbsp bottled artichoke paste, tapenade or pesto

400 g/14 oz canned artichoke hearts, drained

12 thin-cut pancetta rashers

salt and pepper

TO SERVE

rocket leaves

50 g/1³/₄ oz Parmesan or pecorino cheese

2 tbsp olive oil, for drizzling

Grease 6 x 9-cm/3¹/₂-inch loose-based fluted tart tins. To make the pastry, sift the flour and salt into a food processor, add the butter and process until the mixture resembles fine breadcrumbs. Tip into a large bowl. Alternatively, sift the flour and salt into a bowl and rub in the butter with your fingertips until the mixture resembles fine breadcrumbs. Mix in a little iced water, just enough to bring the dough together.

Turn out onto a lightly floured work surface and cut into 6 equal-sized pieces. Roll out each piece and use to line each tart tin, pressing to fit. Roll the rolling pin over the tins to neaten the edges and trim the excess pastry. Put a piece of baking paper into each tartlet and fill with baking beans. Chill for 30 minutes. Meanwhile, preheat the oven to 200°C/400°F/Gas Mark 6.

Bake the tartlet cases in the preheated oven for 10 minutes, then remove the paper and beans.

Meanwhile, to make the filling, stir the cream and artichoke paste together in a bowl and season well with salt and pepper. Divide between the tartlet cases, spreading out to cover the base of each tartlet. Cut each artichoke heart into 3 pieces and divide between the tartlets. Curl 2 rashers of the pancetta into each tart. Bake for 10 minutes.

To serve, top each tartlet with a few rocket leaves. Using a potato peeler, shave the Parmesan cheese and scatter the shavings over the tartlets. Drizzle with oil and serve.

FILO CHICKEN PIE

Put the chicken in a large saucepan and add the onion halves, carrot, celery, bay leaf, lemon rind and peppercorns. Pour in enough cold water to just cover the chicken legs and bring to the boil. Reduce the heat, cover and simmer for 1 hour, or until tender and the juices run clear when a skewer is inserted into the thickest part of the meat. Remove the chicken from the saucepan and leave to cool.

Bring the stock to the boil and boil until reduced to 600 ml/1 pint. Strain and reserve the stock.

When the chicken is cool enough to handle, remove the flesh, discarding the skin and bones. Cut the flesh into bite-sized pieces.

To make the filling, melt 55 g/ 2 oz of the butter in a saucepan over a medium heat. Add the chopped onions and cook, stirring frequently, for 5 minutes, or until softened. Stir in the flour and cook over a low heat, stirring, for 1–2 minutes. Remove from the heat and gradually stir in the reserved stock and the milk. Return to the heat and bring to the boil, stirring constantly, then reduce the heat and simmer for 1–2 minutes until thickened and smooth.

Remove from the heat, stir in the chicken and season to taste with salt and pepper. Leave to cool. Meanwhile, preheat the oven to 190°C/375°F/Gas Mark 5.

When the chicken mixture has cooled, stir in the cheese and eggs and mix together well.

Melt the remaining butter in a saucepan and use a little to lightly grease a deep 30 x 20-cm/12 x 8-inch roasting tin.

Cut the pastry sheets in half widthways. Take one sheet of pastry and cover the remaining sheets with a damp tea towel. Use the sheet to line the tin and brush with a little of the melted butter. Repeat with half the pastry sheets, brushing each with butter.

Spread the chicken filling over the pastry, then top with the remaining pastry sheets, brushing each with butter and tucking down the edges. Using a sharp knife, score the top layers of the pastry into 6 squares.

Bake the pie in a preheated oven for 50 minutes, or until golden brown. Remove from the oven and leave to rest in a warm place for 5–10 minutes, then serve hot, cut into squares.

SERVES 6–8

1 chicken, weighing 1.5 kg/ 3 lb 5 oz

1 small onion, halved, and 3 large onions, finely chopped

1 carrot, thickly sliced

1 celery stick, thickly sliced

1 bay leaf

thinly pared rind of 1 lemon

10 peppercorns

150 g/5¹⁄₂ oz butter

55 g/2 oz plain white flour

150 ml/5 fl oz milk

25 g/1 oz pecorino cheese, grated

3 eggs, beaten

225 g/8 oz filo pastry

salt and pepper

TURKEY PIE

To make the pastry, sift the flour and salt into a bowl. Rub in the margarine and lard with your fingertips until the mixture resembles fine breadcrumbs. Mix in just enough of the iced water to bring the dough together. Wrap in clingfilm and chill for 30 minutes.

Preheat the oven to 190°C/375°F/ Gas Mark 5. Melt half the butter in a saucepan over a medium heat, stir in the flour and cook, stirring constantly, for 1 minute. Gradually whisk in the stock and bring to the boil, whisking constantly. Reduce the heat and simmer for 2 minutes, then stir in the cream. Season to taste with salt and pepper.

Melt the remaining butter in a large frying pan over a low heat. Add the onion and carrots and cook, stirring occasionally, for 5 minutes, or until softened. Add the celery and mushrooms and cook, stirring occasionally, for 5 minutes, then stir in the turkey and peas. Stir into the cream sauce, then transfer to a large pie dish.

Roll out the pastry on a lightly floured work surface to about 3 mm/$\frac{1}{8}$ inch thick. Cut out a rectangle about 2.5 cm/1 inch larger than the dish and lay it over the filling. Crimp the edges, cut 3–4 slits in the top to allow the steam to escape and brush with the beaten egg to glaze. Roll out the trimmings and cut out shapes to decorate the pie, if you like.

Bake the pie in the preheated oven for 30 minutes until golden brown. Serve immediately.

SERVES 6

55 g/2 oz butter

2 tbsp plain flour

225 ml/8 fl oz chicken stock

3 tbsp double cream

1 onion, chopped

2 carrots, sliced

2 celery sticks, chopped

55 g/2 oz mushrooms, sliced

450 g/1 lb cooked turkey, diced

55 g/2 oz frozen peas

1 egg, lightly beaten

salt and pepper

PASTRY

225 g/8 oz plain flour, plus extra for dusting

pinch of salt

115 g/4 oz margarine, diced and chilled

55 g/2 oz lard or white vegetable fat, diced and chilled

1–2 tbsp iced water

GAME PIE

Preheat the oven to 160°C/325°F/ Gas Mark 3. Oil a 1.2-litre/2-pint pie dish. Put the seasoned flour in a large polythene bag, add the meat and shake well to coat each piece.

Heat the oil in a large casserole over a high heat. Add the meat, in batches, and cook until browned all over. Remove with a slotted spoon and keep warm. Add the onion and garlic and cook, stirring, for 2–3 minutes until softened, then add the mushrooms and cook for 2 minutes, stirring constantly, until beginning to wilt. Add the juniper berries, then the port and scrape the sediment from the base of the casserole. Add the stock and bring to the boil, stirring constantly. Leave to bubble for 2–3 minutes. Add the bay leaf and return the meat to the casserole.

Cover, transfer to the preheated oven and cook for 1^1/$_2$–2 hours until the meat is tender. Taste and adjust the seasoning, if necessary. Leave to cool, then chill overnight to develop the flavours. Remove the bay leaf.

Preheat the oven to 200°C/400°F/ Gas Mark 6. Roll out the pastry on a lightly floured work surface to about 7 cm/2^3/$_4$ inches larger than the pie dish. Cut off a 3-cm/1^1/$_4$-inch strip around the edge. Moisten the rim of the dish and press the pastry strip onto it. Put a pie funnel in the centre of the dish and spoon in the meat filling. Don't overfill – and keep any extra gravy to serve separately.

Moisten the pastry collar with a little water and put on the pastry lid. Crimp the edges of the pastry firmly and brush with the beaten egg to glaze.

Bake the pie on a baking sheet near the top of the preheated oven for 30 minutes, or until golden brown and the filling is bubbling hot. Cover with foil and reduce the oven temperature a little if the pastry is getting too brown.

SERVES 4–6

3 tbsp vegetable oil, plus extra for oiling

700 g/1 lb 9 oz mixed game, cut into 3-cm/1^1/$_4$-inch pieces

2 tbsp plain flour, seasoned with salt and pepper, plus extra for dusting

1 onion, roughly chopped

1 garlic clove, finely chopped

350 g/12 oz large field mushrooms, sliced

1 tsp crushed juniper berries

125 ml/4 fl oz port or Marsala

450 ml/16 fl oz chicken or game stock

1 bay leaf

400 g/14 oz ready-made puff pastry, thawed if frozen

1 egg, beaten

RABBIT, ROAST TOMATO AND SAGE PIE

SERVES 4

450 g/1 lb cherry tomatoes

3 tbsp olive oil

$^1/_2$ tsp sugar

1 tbsp plain flour

700 g/1 lb 9 oz boned rabbit, cubed

1 onion, chopped

1 garlic clove, finely chopped

25 g/1 oz pine kernels

150 ml/5 fl oz chicken or vegetable stock

1 tbsp lemon juice

12 fresh sage leaves, finely chopped

35 g/1$^1/_4$ oz butter

100 g/3$^1/_2$ oz filo pastry

salt and pepper

Preheat the oven to 200°C/400°F/Gas Mark 6. Put the tomatoes in a roasting tin and sprinkle with 1 tablespoon of the oil and the sugar. Roast in the preheated oven for 30 minutes.

Meanwhile, put the flour in a polythene bag, add the rabbit and shake well to coat each piece. Heat 1 tablespoon of the remaining oil in a large, heavy-based frying pan over a medium heat. Add the onion and garlic and cook, stirring frequently, for 5 minutes, or until softened. Add the pine kernels and cook, stirring, for 1 minute. Using a slotted spoon, transfer the mixture to a 1.4-litre/2$^1/_2$-pint pie dish.

Heat the remaining oil in the frying pan over a medium–high heat. Add the rabbit and cook until browned all over. Add the stock and lemon juice and bring to the boil, stirring constantly. Reduce the heat and simmer for 2–3 minutes. Transfer the mixture to the pie dish.

When the tomatoes have roasted, gently stir them into the pie dish. Add the sage and season to taste with salt and pepper.

Reduce the oven temperature to 190°C/375°F/Gas Mark 5. Melt the butter in a saucepan over a low heat. Take one sheet of pastry and cover the remaining sheets with a damp tea towel. Brush the sheet with a little of the melted butter, then cut into 2.5-cm/1-inch strips. Arrange on top of the pie. Repeat with the remaining pastry sheets, brushing each with butter and arranging on top of the pie in the opposite direction each time. Make sure that the filling is covered and tuck in the edges.

Bake the pie in the oven for 30 minutes, or until golden brown. Serve hot.

RAISED PORK AND APPLE PIE

To make the filling, cook the potatoes in a saucepan of boiling water for 10 minutes. Drain and set aside. Melt the butter with the oil in a flameproof casserole over a medium–high heat. Add the pork and cook until browned all over. Add the onion and garlic and cook, stirring frequently, for 5 minutes. Stir in the remaining filling ingredients, except the potatoes

and apples. Season to taste with salt and pepper. Reduce the heat, cover and simmer for 1¹/₂ hours. Drain the stock from the casserole and reserve. Leave the pork to cool.

Preheat the oven to 200°C/400°F/ Gas Mark 6. To make the pastry, sift the flour and salt into a bowl. Make a well in the centre. Melt the butter and lard in a saucepan with the water, then bring to the boil. Pour into the well and gradually mix into the flour to form a dough. Turn out onto a lightly floured surface and knead until smooth. Reserve a quarter of the dough and use the remainder to line the base and side of a large pie tin or deep 20-cm/ 8-inch round loose-based cake tin.

Layer the pork, potatoes and apples in the base. Roll out the reserved pastry to make a lid. Dampen the edges and put the lid on top, sealing well. Brush with the beaten egg to glaze. Make a hole in the top. Bake in the preheated oven for 30 minutes, then reduce the temperature to 160°C/325°F/Gas Mark 3 and bake for a further 45 minutes. Dissolve the gelatine in the reserved stock and pour into the hole in the lid as the pie cools. Serve well chilled.

SERVES 8

FILLING

900 g/2 lb waxy potatoes, sliced

2 tbsp butter

2 tbsp vegetable oil

450 g/1 lb lean boneless pork, cubed

2 onions, sliced

4 garlic cloves, crushed

4 tbsp tomato purée

600 ml/1 pint stock

2 tbsp chopped fresh sage

2 eating apples, peeled, cored and sliced

salt and pepper

PASTRY

675 g/1 lb 8 oz plain flour, plus extra for dusting

pinch of salt

4 tbsp butter

125 g/4¹/₂ oz lard

300 m/10 fl oz water

1 egg, beaten

1 tsp gelatine

POTATO AND HAM PIE

SERVES 12

225 g/8 oz waxy potatoes, cubed

2 tbsp butter

8 shallots, halved

225 g/8 oz smoked ham, cubed

2½ tbsp plain flour

300 ml/10 fl oz milk

2 tbsp wholegrain mustard

50 g/1¾ oz pineapple, cubed

salt and pepper

PASTRY

225 g/8 oz plain flour, plus extra for dusting

½ tsp mustard powder

pinch of salt

pinch of cayenne pepper

150 g/5½ oz butter, diced and chilled

125 g/4½ oz mature Cheddar cheese, grated

2 egg yolks, plus extra for glazing

4–6 tsp iced water

Cook the potato cubes in a saucepan of boiling water for 10 minutes. Drain and set aside.

Meanwhile, melt the butter in a separate saucepan over a low heat. Add the shallots and cook, stirring frequently, for 3–4 minutes until beginning to brown.

Add the ham and cook, stirring, for 2–3 minutes. Stir in the flour and cook, stirring, for 1 minute. Gradually stir in the milk. Add the mustard and pineapple and bring to the boil, stirring. Season well with salt and pepper and add the potato.

Preheat the oven to 190°C/375°F/ Gas Mark 5. To make the pastry, sift the flour, mustard powder, salt and cayenne pepper into a bowl. Rub in the butter with your fingertips until the mixture resembles fine

breadcrumbs. Stir in the cheese. Add the egg yolks and water and mix to form a dough. Turn out onto a lightly floured work surface. Cut the pastry in half. Roll out one half and use to line a shallow pie dish.

Spoon the filling into the pie dish. Brush the edges with water. Roll out the remaining pastry and press it on top of the pie, sealing the edges. Decorate with the trimmings. Brush with egg yolk to glaze and bake in the preheated oven for 40–45 minutes, or until golden brown.

ROSEMARY LAMB IN FILO PASTRY

Heat 2 tablespoons of the oil in a heavy-based saucepan over a medium heat. Add the onion and garlic and cook, stirring frequently, for 5 minutes, or until the onion is softened. Add the spinach and nutmeg and cook, stirring, for 3 minutes.

Turn into a food processor or blender, add the yogurt and salt and pepper to taste and process until smooth. Leave the mixture to cool.

Meanwhile, heat the remaining oil in a frying pan over a medium–high heat. Add the lamb fillets and rosemary and cook for 3 minutes on each side. Remove from the frying pan, drain on kitchen paper and leave to cool.

Preheat the oven to 190°C/375°F/ Gas Mark 5. When the lamb fillets are cool, slash each fillet 4 times,

almost all the way through. Fill each slash with the spinach mixture, spreading any remaining mixture on top. Season the fillets to taste with salt and pepper.

Melt the butter in a saucepan over a low heat. Take one sheet of pastry and cover the remaining sheets with a damp tea towel. Brush the sheet with a little of the melted butter. Put a second sheet on top, brush with butter and fold both sheets in half. Put a lamb fillet in the centre and wrap to form a parcel. Put on a baking sheet and brush with butter. Repeat with the remaining pastry and lamb fillets to form 4 parcels.

Bake the lamb parcels in the preheated oven for 25 minutes until golden. Serve hot.

SERVES 4

3 tbsp olive oil

1 small onion, finely chopped

1 garlic clove, finely chopped

175 g/6 oz spinach leaves

pinch of freshly grated nutmeg

2 tbsp Greek yogurt

4 lamb fillets, about 115 g/4 oz each

1 tsp finely chopped fresh rosemary leaves

70 g/2¹/₂ oz butter

8 sheets filo pastry

salt and pepper

PORK FILLET (TENDERLOIN) CAN BE USED IN EXACTLY THE SAME WAY AS THE LAMB AND, INSTEAD OF THE SPINACH PURÉE, YOU COULD USE A LEEK PURÉE WITH EITHER MEAT. PREPARE THIS IN THE SAME WAY AS THE SPINACH PURÉE IN THE RECIPE, BUT SUBSTITUTE THE SPINACH LEAVES WITH THE SAME QUANTITY OF SLICED LEEKS AND COOK FOR 10 MINUTES UNTIL TENDER.

SHEPHERD'S PIE

SERVES 6

1 tbsp olive oil

2 onions, finely chopped

2 garlic cloves, finely chopped

675 g/1 lb 8 oz good-quality fresh lamb mince

2 carrots, finely chopped

1 tbsp plain flour

225 ml/8 fl oz beef or chicken stock

125 ml/4 fl oz full-bodied red wine

Worcestershire sauce (optional)

salt and pepper

MASHED POTATOES

675 g/1 lb 8 oz floury potatoes, such as King Edwards, Maris Piper or Desirée, peeled and cut into chunks

55 g/2 oz butter

2 tbsp cream or milk

salt and pepper

Preheat the oven to 180°C/350°F/ Gas Mark 4. Heat the oil in a large casserole over a medium heat. Add the onions and cook, stirring frequently, for 5 minutes, or until softened. Stir in the garlic. Increase the heat, add the mince and cook, stirring constantly with a wooden spoon to break up the meat, until browned all over. Add the carrots and season well with salt and pepper.

Stir in the flour and add the stock and wine. Bring to the boil, stirring, then reduce the heat and simmer until thickened.

Cover the casserole, transfer to the preheated oven and cook for 1 hour. Check the consistency from time to time and add a little more stock or wine, if necessary. The meat mixture

should be quite thick, but not dry. Season to taste with salt and pepper and add a little Worcestershire sauce, if you like.

Meanwhile, cook the potatoes in a large saucepan of boiling salted water for 15–20 minutes, then drain well. Mash with a potato masher until smooth. Beat in the butter and cream and season well with salt and pepper.

Spoon the lamb mixture into an ovenproof serving dish and spread or pipe the potato on top.

Increase the oven temperature to 200°C/400°F/Gas Mark 6 and bake the pie at the top of the oven for 15–20 minutes until golden brown. Finish off under a medium grill for a really crisp brown potato topping.

POTATO, BEEF AND LEEK PASTIES

Preheat the oven to 200°C/400°F/ Gas Mark 6. Lightly grease a baking sheet. Mix the potatoes, carrot, beef and leek together in a large bowl. Season well with salt and pepper.

Divide the pastry into 4 equal-sized pieces. Roll out each piece on a lightly floured work surface into a 20-cm/8-inch round.

Spoon the potato mixture onto one half of each round, to within 1 cm/$\frac{1}{2}$ inch of the edge. Top the potato mixture with the butter, dividing it equally between the rounds. Brush the pastry edge with

a little of the beaten egg. Fold the pastry over to encase the filling and crimp the edges together to seal.

Transfer the pasties to the prepared baking sheet and brush with the beaten egg to glaze.

Bake in the preheated oven for 20 minutes. Reduce the temperature to 160°C/325°F/Gas Mark 3 and bake for a further 30 minutes, or until golden brown.

Serve the pasties hot or warm.

SERVES 4

butter, for greasing

225 g/8 oz waxy potatoes, diced

1 small carrot, diced

225 g/8 oz beef steak, cubed

1 leek, sliced

225 g/8 oz ready-made shortcrust pastry, thawed if frozen

plain flour, for dusting

1 tbsp butter

1 egg, beaten

salt and pepper

USE OTHER TYPES OF MEAT, SUCH AS PORK OR CHICKEN, IN THE PASTIES AND ADD CHUNKS OF APPLE TO THE FILLING, IF PREFERRED.

CARROT-TOPPED BEEF PIE

SERVES 4

450 g/1 lb fresh beef mince

1 onion, chopped

1 garlic clove, crushed

1 tbsp plain flour

300 ml/10 fl oz beef stock

2 tbsp tomato purée

1 celery stick, chopped

3 tbsp chopped fresh parsley

1 tbsp Worcestershire sauce

675 g/1 lb 8 oz floury
potatoes, diced

2 large carrots, diced

25 g/1 oz butter

3 tbsp milk

salt and pepper

Heat a large saucepan over a high heat. Add the mince and dry-fry for 3–4 minutes, stirring constantly with a wooden spoon to break up the meat, until browned all over. Add the onion and garlic and cook, stirring frequently, for 5 minutes, or until the onion is softened.

Add the flour and cook, stirring, for 1 minute. Gradually blend in the stock and tomato purée. Stir in the celery, 1 tablespoon of the parsley and the Worcestershire sauce. Season to taste with salt and pepper.

Bring the mixture to the boil, then reduce the heat and simmer for 20–25 minutes. Spoon into a 1.2-litre/2-pint pie dish. Preheat the oven to 190°C/375°F/Gas Mark 5.

Meanwhile, cook the potatoes and carrots in a saucepan of boiling water for 10 minutes. Drain and mash them together.

Beat the butter, milk and the remaining parsley into the potato and carrot mixture and season to taste with salt and pepper. Spread or pipe the potato and carrot mixture on top of the meat mixture.

Bake in the preheated oven for 45 minutes, or until cooked through and golden brown on top. Serve hot.

You can use fresh lamb, turkey or pork mince instead of the beef, adding appropriate herbs, such as rosemary and sage, for added flavour.

STEAK AND KIDNEY PIE

Preheat the oven to 160°C/325°F/ Gas Mark 3. Grease a 1.2-litre/2-pint pie dish.

Put the flour with salt and pepper to taste in a large polythene bag, add the steak and kidney and shake well to coat each piece.

Heat the oil in a flameproof casserole over a high heat. Add the steak and kidney, in batches, and cook until browned all over. Remove with a slotted spoon and keep warm. Add the onion and garlic to the casserole and cook, stirring, for 2–3 minutes until softened.

Stir in the wine and scrape the sediment from the base of the casserole. Pour in the stock and bring to the boil, stirring constantly. Leave to bubble for 2–3 minutes. Add the bay leaf and return the meat to the casserole.

Cover, transfer to the centre of the preheated oven and cook for 1½–2 hours. Taste and adjust the seasoning, if necessary. Leave to

cool, then preferably chill overnight to develop the flavours. Remove the bay leaf.

Preheat the oven to 200°C/400°F/ Gas Mark 6. Roll out the pastry on a lightly floured work surface to about 7 cm/2³⁄₄ inches larger than the pie dish. Cut off a 3-cm/1¹⁄₄-inch strip from the edge. Moisten the rim of the dish and press the pastry strip onto it. Put a pie funnel in the centre of the dish and spoon in the steak and kidney filling. Don't overfill – keep any extra gravy to serve separately. Moisten the pastry collar with water and put on the pastry lid. Crimp the edges of the pastry firmly. Brush with the beaten egg to glaze.

Bake the pie on a baking sheet near the top of the preheated oven for 30 minutes, or until golden brown and the filling is bubbling hot. Cover with foil and reduce the oven temperature a little if the pastry is getting too brown.

SERVES 4–6

butter, for greasing

2 tbsp plain flour, plus extra for dusting

700 g/1 lb 9 oz braising steak, trimmed and cut into 4-cm/ 1¹⁄₂-inch cubes

3 lamb's kidneys, skinned, cored and cut into 2.5-cm/ 1-inch pieces

3 tbsp vegetable oil

1 onion, roughly chopped

1 garlic clove, finely chopped

125 ml/4 fl oz full-bodied red wine

450 ml/16 fl oz stock

1 bay leaf

400 g/14 oz ready-made puff pastry, thawed if frozen

1 egg, beaten

salt and pepper

SOME PEOPLE USE SHORTCRUST PASTRY FOR THIS TRADITIONAL BRITISH PIE, BUT THE RICHER PUFF PASTRY IS BETTER AS IT GIVES A REALLY CRISP CRUST WHILE ALLOWING THE BASE OF THE PASTRY TO ABSORB SOME OF THE GRAVY AND HENCE HAVE A BETTER FLAVOUR. THERE ARE REGIONAL VARIATIONS OF STEAK AND KIDNEY PIE, WITH SOME COOKS ADDING MUSHROOMS AND OYSTERS TO THE FILLING.

BEEF WELLINGTON

SERVES 4

750 g/1 lb 10 oz thick beef fillet

2 tbsp butter

2 tbsp vegetable oil

1 garlic clove, chopped

1 onion, chopped

175 g/6 oz chestnut mushrooms

1 tbsp chopped fresh sage

350 g/12 oz frozen puff pastry, thawed

plain flour, for dusting

1 egg, beaten

salt and pepper

Preheat the oven to 220°C/425°F/ Gas Mark 7. Put the beef in a roasting tin, spread with the butter and season to taste with salt and pepper. Roast in the preheated oven for 30 minutes. Meanwhile, heat the oil in a saucepan over a medium heat. Add the garlic and onion and cook, stirring, for 3 minutes. Add the mushrooms, sage and salt and pepper to taste and cook, stirring frequently, for 5 minutes. Remove from the heat.

Roll out the pastry on a lightly floured work surface into a rectangle large enough to enclose the beef. Put the beef in the centre and spread over the mushroom mixture. Bring the long sides of the pastry together over the beef and seal with the beaten egg. Tuck the short ends over (trim away the excess pastry) and seal. Put, seam-side down, on a baking sheet. Make 2 slits in the top. Decorate with pastry trimmings and brush with the beaten egg to glaze.

Bake in the oven for 40 minutes. Cut into thick slices to serve.

STEAK AND MUSHROOM PIE

Preheat the oven to 160°C/325°F/Gas Mark 3. Put 2 tablespoons of the flour in a large polythene bag, with salt and pepper to taste, add the meat – shake well to coat.

Heat the oil in a flameproof casserole over a high heat and cook the meat until brown. Brown the meat in batches. Remove it from the dish with a slotted spoon and keep it warm.

Fry the onion and garlic in the casserole dish over a medium heat for 2–3 minutes until softened and then add the mushrooms. Continue to cook for about 2 minutes, stirring constantly, until they start to shrink.

Carefully stir in the wine and scrape the bottom of the pan to release all the sediment. Pour in the stock, stirring constantly, and bring to the boil – let the mixture simmer for 2–3 minutes.

Add the bay leaf and return the meat to the casserole. Cover and cook in the centre of the preheated oven for 1½–2 hours until the meat is tender. Check the seasoning and adjust if necessary.

Remove from the oven, discard the bay leaf and allow to cool in a refrigerator, preferably overnight (this allows the flavours to develop).

Preheat the oven to 200°C/400°F/Gas Mark 6. Roll out the pastry on a lightly floured work surface to about 5 cm/2 inches larger than the pie dish (use the inverted dish as a measure). Cut off a strip, 1 cm/½ inch wide, from around the edge. Moisten the rim of the dish with water and press the pastry strip onto it. Place a pie funnel in the centre of the dish and spoon in the steak and mushroom filling. Do not overfill, and keep any extra gravy to serve separately.

Moisten the pastry collar with a little water and put on the pastry lid, taking care to fit it carefully round the pie funnel. Crimp the edges of the pastry firmly and glaze with the beaten egg. You can use some leftover dough to make leaf shapes to garnish the pie – stick these on using the beaten egg and glaze well with egg.

Place the pie on a baking sheet and bake near the top of the preheated oven for 30 minutes, or until golden brown. If the pastry is getting too brown, cover it with foil and reduce the oven temperature to 180°C/350°F/Gas Mark 4. The pie should be golden brown and the filling bubbling hot.

SERVES 4–6

4 tbsp plain flour

700 g/1 lb 9 oz braising steak, cut into 4 cm/1½ inch pieces

3 tbsp vegetable oil

1 onion, roughly chopped

1 garlic clove, finely chopped

350 g/12 oz mushrooms, wiped and sliced

125 ml/4 fl oz full-bodied red wine

450 ml/16 fl oz beef stock

1 bay leaf

400 g/14 oz ready-made puff pastry, thawed if frozen

1 egg, beaten

salt and pepper

8

BARBECUE

Cook over a barbecue to enjoy the natural flavours of meat at its best, when the mild smokiness and caramelized meat sugars simply melt in your mouth. All types of meat can be cooked on a barbecue but, just as in in other fast cooking techniques such as grilling or frying, the cuts that work best are steaks, cubed lean meat, chops, sausages and burgers. The golden rule of barbecuing is always to cook over embers rather than flames – this stops the meat from becoming unpleasantly carbonized. Try out Sherried Chicken Liver Brochettes, Fruity Duck or Turkish Kebabs for a delicious change from steaks and sausages.

ITALIAN DEVILLED CHICKEN

Put the chicken cubes in a large, shallow, non-metallic dish. Put the oil, lemon rind and juice, garlic and chillies in a jug and stir together until well blended. Season to taste with salt and pepper. Pour over the chicken and turn gently to coat in the marinade. Cover and leave to marinate in the refrigerator for up to 8 hours.

Preheat the barbecue. Remove the chicken from the marinade, reserving the marinade. Thread the chicken onto several presoaked wooden skewers and cook over medium-hot coals, turning frequently and brushing with the marinade, but not for the last 5 minutes of the cooking time, for 10 minutes, or until the chicken is cooked through.

Transfer to a large serving dish, garnish with parsley sprigs and serve immediately.

SERVES 4

4 skinless, boneless chicken breasts, about 175 g/6 oz each, cut into 2.5-cm/1-inch cubes

125 ml/4 fl oz olive oil

finely grated rind and juice of 1 lemon

2 garlic cloves, finely chopped

2 tsp finely chopped fresh red chillies

salt and pepper

fresh flat-leaf parsley sprigs, to garnish

YOU CAN ALSO MAKE THESE KEBABS WITH DARK CHICKEN MEAT, SUCH AS SKINLESS, BONELESS THIGHS.

SHERRIED CHICKEN LIVER BROCHETTES

Cut the chicken livers into 5-cm/2-inch pieces. Combine the ingredients for the marinade in a shallow dish. Add the chicken livers and toss to coat in the marinade. Cover and leave to marinate in the refrigerator for 3–4 hours.

Mix the mustard and mayonnaise together in a bowl, cover and chill until required.

Preheat the barbecue. Cut each rasher in half. Put on a chopping board and use the back of a knife to stretch gently until almost double in length. Remove the chicken livers from the marinade, reserving the marinade. Wrap the bacon rashers around half of the chicken liver pieces. Thread the bacon and chicken liver rolls and the plain chicken liver pieces alternately onto 6 presoaked wooden skewers.

Cook over hot coals, turning frequently and brushing with the marinade, but not for the last 5 minutes of the cooking time, for 10–12 minutes until cooked through.

Meanwhile, cut each bread half into 3 pieces and toast the cut sides on the barbecue until golden brown.

To serve, top the toasted bread with the spinach and put the kebabs on top. Spoon over the mayonnaise.

SERVES 6

400 g/14 oz chicken livers, cored and trimmed

3 rindless streaky bacon rashers

1 ciabatta loaf or small French stick, halved horizontally

225 g/8 oz baby spinach leaves, washed

MARINADE

150 ml/5 fl oz dry sherry

4 tbsp olive oil

1 tsp wholegrain mustard

salt and pepper, to taste

MUSTARD MAYONNAISE

8 tbsp mayonnaise

1 tsp wholegrain mustard

TAKE CARE NOT TO OVERCOOK THE CHICKEN LIVERS OR THEY WILL BECOME TOUGH. THEY SHOULD BE FIRM TO THE TOUCH AND JUST PINK INSIDE.

BARBECUED CHICKEN

SERVES 4

1 litre/1³/₄ pints chicken stock

8 chicken thighs

1 tbsp lime juice

2 garlic cloves, crushed

2 tbsp Thai soy sauce

1 tbsp Thai fish sauce

2 tbsp chilli sauce

lime wedges, to garnish

Bring the stock to the boil in a large wok. Add the chicken, reduce the heat and simmer for 8–10 minutes until cooked. Remove with a slotted spoon and leave to cool.

When cold, put the chicken in a shallow, non-metallic dish. Combine the lime juice, garlic, soy sauce, fish sauce and chilli sauce in a bowl and spoon over the chicken, turning to coat in the marinade. Cover and leave to marinate in the refrigerator for 2–3 hours. Preheat the barbecue.

Remove the chicken from the marinade, reserving the marinade. Cook the chicken over hot coals, turning frequently and brushing with the marinade, but not for the last 5 minutes of the cooking time, for 8–10 minutes until browned and crisp. Serve the chicken hot or cold, garnished with lime wedges.

YOU CAN ALSO COOK THE CHICKEN UNDER THE GRILL OR ON A RIDGED GRIDDLE PAN. IT IS IMPORTANT THAT THE MEAT IS COOKED ALL THE WAY THROUGH – THIS IS WHY IT IS COOKED BEFORE BARBECUING. DON'T FORGET THAT REHEATING MEAT THOROUGHLY IS JUST AS IMPORTANT AS COOKING IT THOROUGHLY.

SERVES 4

4 chicken drumsticks

4 chicken thighs

2 fresh corn on the cob, husks and silks removed

85 g/3 oz butter, melted

SPICE MIX

2 tsp onion powder

2 tsp paprika

1¹/₂ tsp salt

1 tsp garlic powder

1 tsp dried thyme

1 tsp cayenne pepper

1 tsp ground black pepper

¹/₂ tsp ground white pepper

¹/₄ tsp ground cumin

CAJUN CHICKEN

Preheat the barbecue. Using a sharp knife, make 2 or 3 diagonal slashes in the chicken drumsticks and thighs, then put in a large dish. Cut the corn on the cob into thick slices and add to the dish. Mix all the ingredients for the spice mix together in a small bowl.

Brush the chicken and corn with the melted butter and sprinkle with the spice mix. Toss to coat well.

Cook the chicken over medium-hot coals, turning occasionally, for 15 minutes, then add the corn slices and cook, turning occasionally, for a further 10–15 minutes, or until beginning to blacken slightly at the edges. Transfer to a large serving plate and serve immediately.

To remove the husks from the corn on the cob, gently pull them away from the corn towards the base, then cut off the base and remove the silks.

219

SAGE AND LEMON POUSSINS

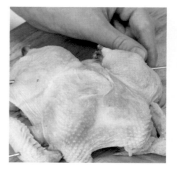

Preheat the barbecue. To spatchcock the poussins, turn one bird, breast-side down, and, using strong kitchen scissors or poultry shears, cut through the skin and ribcage along both sides of the backbone, from tail to neck. Remove the backbone and turn the bird breast-side up. Press down firmly on the breastbone with the heel of your hand to flatten. Fold the wingtips underneath. Repeat with the remaining poussins.

Thinly slice half the lemon and finely grate the rind of the other half. Mix the lemon rind and sage together in a small bowl. Loosen the skin on the breasts and legs of the poussins and insert the lemon and sage mixture. Tuck in the lemon slices and smooth the skin back firmly. Push a metal skewer through one wing, the top of the breast and the other wing. Push a second skewer through one thigh, the bottom of the breast and the other thigh. Season to taste with salt and pepper.

Cook the poussins over medium-hot coals for 10–15 minutes on each side. Serve garnished with herb sprigs and lemon slices.

SERVES 4

4 poussins, about 450 g/ 1 lb each

1 lemon

2 tbsp chopped fresh sage

salt and pepper

TO GARNISH

fresh herb sprigs

lemon slices

YOU CAN THREAD THE SKEWERS CROSSWAYS THROUGH THE POUSSIN. PUSH A SKEWER THROUGH A WING AND OUT THROUGH THE THIGH ON THE OPPOSITE SIDE. REPEAT WITH THE OTHER SKEWER ON THE OTHER SIDE.

FRUITY DUCK

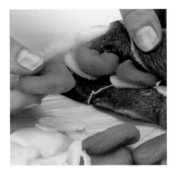

SERVES 4

4 duck breasts, about 175 g/
6 oz each

115 g/4 oz ready-to-eat
dried apricots

2 shallots, thinly sliced

2 tbsp clear honey

1 tsp sesame oil

2 tsp Chinese five-spice powder

4 spring onion tassels, to
garnish

Preheat the barbecue. Using a sharp knife, cut a long slit in the fleshy side of each duck breast to make a pocket. Divide the apricots and shallots between the pockets and secure with skewers.

Mix the honey and sesame oil together in a small bowl and brush all over the duck breasts. Sprinkle the duck breasts all over with the five-spice powder.

To make the garnish, make a few cuts lengthways down each spring onion. Put in a bowl of iced water and leave until the tassels open out. Drain well before using.

Cook the duck breasts over medium-hot coals for 6–8 minutes on each side. Remove the skewers, transfer to a large serving plate and garnish with the spring onion tassels. Serve immediately.

SPICY TURKEY AND CHORIZO KEBABS

Put the oil, garlic, chilli and salt and pepper to taste in a small screw-top jar, screw the lid on tightly and shake well to combine. Leave to stand for 1 hour for the garlic and chilli to flavour the oil.

Preheat the barbecue. Using a sharp knife, cut the turkey into 2.5-cm/1-inch pieces. Cut the chorizo into 2.5-cm/1-inch lengths. Core the apple and cut into chunks. Sprinkle the apple with the lemon juice to prevent discoloration.

Thread the turkey and chorizo pieces onto 8 metal skewers, alternating with the apple chunks and bay leaves.

Cook the kebabs over hot coals, turning and basting frequently with the flavoured oil, for 15 minutes, or until the turkey is cooked through.

Transfer the kebabs to warmed serving plates and serve immediately.

SERVES 8

6 tbsp olive oil

2 garlic cloves, crushed

1 fresh red chilli, deseeded and chopped

350 g/12 oz turkey breast fillet

300 g/10^1/$_2$ oz chorizo sausage

1 eating apple

1 tbsp lemon juice

8 bay leaves

salt and pepper

THE FLAVOURED OIL FEATURED IN THIS RECIPE CAN BE USED TO BASTE ANY GRILLED MEAT, GIVING IT A SUBTLE CHILLI FLAVOUR. IT WILL KEEP IN THE REFRIGERATOR FOR ABOUT 2 WEEKS.

CHINESE RIBS

Put the spare ribs in a large, shallow, non-metallic dish. Mix the soy sauce, sugar, oil, garlic, five-spice powder and ginger together in a bowl. Pour the mixture over the ribs and turn until coated in the marinade. Cover and leave to marinate in the refrigerator for at least 6 hours.

Preheat the barbecue. Remove the ribs from the marinade, reserving the marinade. Cook over medium-hot coals, turning frequently and brushing with the reserved marinade, but not for the last 10 minutes of the cooking time, for 30–40 minutes.

Transfer to a large serving dish, garnish with the shredded spring onions and serve immediately.

SERVES 4

1 kg/2 lb 4 oz pork spare ribs, separated

4 tbsp dark soy sauce

3 tbsp muscovado sugar

1 tbsp groundnut or sunflower oil

2 garlic cloves, finely chopped

2 tsp Chinese five-spice powder

1-cm/^{1}/$_2$-inch piece fresh root ginger, grated

shredded spring onions, to garnish

PIGS IN BLANKETS

Preheat the barbecue. Thinly slice the mozzarella cheese. Using a sharp knife, cut a deep slit in the side of each sausage. Spread the cut sides with the mustard. Divide the slices of cheese between the sausages and reshape.

Put the bacon rashers on a chopping board and use the back of a knife to stretch gently until almost double in length. Wrap one rasher tightly around each sausage.

Cook over hot coals, turning frequently, for 15–20 minutes until cooked through. Transfer to a large serving plate and serve immediately.

SERVES 4

115 g/4 oz mozzarella cheese

8 Toulouse sausages

2 tbsp Dijon mustard

8 smoked bacon rashers

TOULOUSE SAUSAGES ARE FAIRLY LARGE COOKING SAUSAGES MADE FROM ROUGHLY CHOPPED PORK. THEY ARE WIDELY AVAILABLE, BUT YOU CAN SUBSTITUTE OTHER GOOD-QUALITY COOKING SAUSAGES. SECURE THE BACON RASHERS AROUND THE SAUSAGES WITH WOODEN COCKTAIL STICKS, IF NECESSARY.

NORMANDY BROCHETTES

Using a sharp knife, cut the pork into 2.5-cm/1-inch cubes, then put in a large, shallow, non-metallic dish. Mix the cider, sage and peppercorns together in a jug, pour over the pork cubes and turn to coat in the marinade. Cover and leave to marinate in the refrigerator for 1–2 hours.

Preheat the barbecue. Remove the pork from the marinade, reserving the marinade. Core the apples, but do not peel, and cut into wedges. Dip the apple wedges into the reserved marinade and thread onto several metal skewers, alternating with the cubes of pork. Stir the sunflower oil into the remaining marinade.

Cook the brochettes over medium-hot coals, turning frequently and brushing with the marinade, but not for the last 5 minutes of the cooking time, for 12–15 minutes. Transfer to a large serving plate and serve immediately.

SERVES 4

450 g/1 lb pork fillet

300 ml/10 fl oz dry cider

1 tbsp finely chopped fresh sage

6 black peppercorns, crushed

2 crisp eating apples

1 tbsp sunflower oil

REPLACE 1 APPLE WITH 6 READY-TO-EAT PRUNES WRAPPED IN STRIPS OF STREAKY BACON. THREAD THE PRUNES ONTO THE SKEWERS WITH THE REMAINING APPLE AND PORK.

SAUSAGES WITH BARBECUE SAUCE

To make the sauce, heat the oil in a small saucepan over a medium heat. Add the onion and garlic and cook, stirring frequently, for 4–5 minutes until the onion is softened.

Add the tomatoes with their juice, the Worcestershire sauce, brown fruity sauce, sugar, vinegar, chilli powder, mustard powder, Tabasco sauce and salt and pepper to taste. Bring to the boil, stirring.

Reduce the heat to low and simmer gently, stirring occasionally, for 10–15 minutes, or until beginning to thicken slightly. Keep warm until required.

Preheat the barbecue. Cook the sausages over hot coals, turning frequently, for 10–15 minutes until cooked through. Do not prick the sausages with a fork or the juices and fat will run out and cause the barbecue to flare.

Put each sausage in a bread finger roll and serve immediately with the barbecue sauce.

SERVES 4

2 tbsp sunflower oil

1 large onion, chopped

2 cloves garlic, chopped

225 g/8 oz canned chopped tomatoes in juice

1 tbsp Worcestershire sauce

2 tbsp brown fruity sauce

2 tbsp light muscovado sugar

4 tbsp white wine vinegar

$^1\!/_2$ tsp mild chilli powder

$^1\!/_4$ tsp mustard powder

dash of Tabasco sauce

450 g/1 lb sausages

salt and pepper

bread finger rolls, to serve

TURKISH KEBABS

SERVES 4

500 g/1 lb 2 oz boned
shoulder of lamb, cut into
2.5-cm/1-inch cubes

1 tbsp olive oil

2 tbsp dry white wine

2 tbsp finely chopped
fresh mint

4 garlic cloves, finely chopped

2 tsp grated orange rind

1 tbsp paprika

1 tsp sugar

salt and pepper

TAHINI CREAM

225 g/8 oz tahini paste

2 garlic cloves, finely chopped

2 tbsp extra virgin olive oil

2 tbsp lemon juice

125 ml/4 fl oz water

Put the lamb cubes in a large, shallow, non-metallic dish. Mix the oil, wine, mint, garlic, orange rind, paprika and sugar together in a jug and season to taste with salt and pepper. Pour over the lamb and turn to coat in the marinade. Cover and leave to marinate in the refrigerator for 2 hours, turning occasionally.

Preheat the barbecue. To make the tahini cream, put the tahini paste, garlic, oil and lemon juice in a food processor and process briefly to mix. With the motor still running, gradually add the water through the feed tube until smooth. Transfer to a bowl, cover and chill until required.

Remove the lamb from the marinade, reserving the marinade. Thread onto several long metal skewers. Cook over medium-hot coals, turning frequently and brushing with the marinade, but not for the last 5 minutes of the cooking time, for 10–15 minutes, or until cooked through.

Serve the kebabs immediately with the tahini cream.

TAHINI, OR SESAME SEED PASTE, IS AVAILABLE FROM MOST SUPERMARKETS AND SPECIALIST FOOD SHOPS. IT IS MADE FROM GROUND, PULPED SESAME SEEDS.

SPICY RACK OF LAMB WITH HUMMUS

Preheat the oven to 190°C/375°F/ Gas Mark 5. Put the lamb in a roasting tin and spoon over the oil. Roast in the preheated oven for 10–15 minutes, or until almost cooked through.

Mix all the ingredients for the marinade together in a small bowl. Brush the spice mixture all over the warm lamb, then transfer to a dish and leave to cool completely. Cover and leave to marinate in the refrigerator overnight.

Preheat the barbecue. Cook the lamb over medium-hot coals, turning frequently, until heated through and well browned. Transfer to 6 serving plates and add 2–3 tablespoons hummus to each. Garnish with mint sprigs and serve.

SERVES 6

6 racks of lamb, each with 3 cutlets

2 tbsp olive oil

few fresh mint sprigs, to garnish

ready-made hummus, to serve

MARINADE

1 tbsp olive oil

2 tbsp clear honey

2 tsp ground coriander

2 tsp ground cumin

1 tsp ground allspice

$\frac{1}{2}$ tsp paprika

BEEFBURGERS WITH CHILLI AND BASIL

SERVES 4

650 g/1 lb 7 oz fresh
beef mince

1 red pepper, deseeded and
finely chopped

1 garlic clove, finely chopped

2 small fresh red chillies,
deseeded and finely chopped

1 tbsp chopped fresh basil, plus
extra sprigs to garnish

$^1/_2$ tsp ground cumin

salt and pepper

hamburger buns, to serve

Preheat the barbecue. Put the mince, red pepper, garlic, chillies, chopped basil and cumin in a bowl and mix until well combined. Season the mixture to taste with salt and pepper.

With wet hands, form the mixture into burger shapes. Cook the burgers over hot coals for 5–8 minutes on each side, or until cooked through.

Serve immediately in hamburger buns, garnished with basil sprigs.

MUSTARD STEAKS WITH TOMATO RELISH

To make the tomato relish, put all the ingredients in a heavy-based saucepan and season to taste with salt. Bring to the boil, stirring until the sugar has completely dissolved. Reduce the heat and simmer, stirring occasionally, for 40 minutes, or until thickened. Transfer to a bowl, cover and leave to cool.

Preheat the barbecue. Using a sharp knife, cut almost completely through each steak horizontally to make a pocket. Spread the mustard inside the pockets and rub the steaks all over with the garlic. Put on a plate, cover and leave to stand in a cool place for 30 minutes.

Cook the steaks over hot coals for 2$^{1}/_{2}$ minutes each side for rare, 4 minutes each side for medium or 6 minutes each side for well done.

Transfer to warmed serving plates, garnish with tarragon sprigs and serve immediately with the tomato relish.

SERVES 4

4 sirloin or rump steaks

1 tbsp tarragon mustard

2 garlic cloves, crushed

fresh tarragon sprigs, to garnish

TOMATO RELISH

225 g/8 oz cherry tomatoes

55 g/2 oz muscovado sugar

50 ml/2 fl oz white wine vinegar

1 piece stem ginger, chopped

$^{1}/_{2}$ lime, thinly sliced

salt

USE LONG-HANDLED TONGS TO TURN THE STEAKS OVER. TRY TO AVOID USING A FORK, AS THIS WILL PIERCE THE MEAT AND SOME OF THE DELICIOUS JUICES WILL BE LOST.

BEEF SATAY

Using a sharp knife, cut the steak into 2.5-cm/1-inch cubes, then put in a large, shallow, non-metallic dish. Mix the honey, soy sauce, oil, garlic, coriander, caraway seeds and chilli powder together in a small jug. Pour over the steak and turn to coat in the marinade. Cover and leave to marinate in the refrigerator for 2 hours, turning occasionally. Preheat the barbecue.

Remove the steak from the marinade, reserving the marinade. Thread onto several presoaked wooden skewers.

Cook over hot coals, turning frequently and brushing with the marinade, but not for the last 5 minutes of the cooking time, for 8 minutes, or until cooked through. Transfer to a large serving plate, garnish with lime wedges and serve.

SERVES 6

1 kg/2 lb 4 oz rump steak

1 tbsp clear honey

2 tbsp dark soy sauce

2 tbsp groundnut oil

1 garlic clove, finely chopped

1 tsp ground coriander

1 tsp caraway seeds

pinch of chilli powder

lime wedges, to garnish

INSTEAD OF CUTTING THE STEAK INTO SMALL CUBES, SLICE IT INTO LONG, NARROW STRIPS AND THREAD THE STRIPS CONCERTINA-STYLE ONTO THE SKEWERS.

THAI-SPICED BEEF AND PEPPER KEBABS

SERVES 4

4 tbsp rice wine or dry sherry

75 ml/2^1/$_2$ fl oz soy sauce

75 ml/2^1/$_2$ fl oz hoisin sauce

3 cloves garlic, finely chopped

1 fresh red chilli, deseeded and finely chopped

1^1/$_2$ tbsp grated fresh root ginger

3 spring onions, finely chopped

salt and pepper

KEBABS

1 kg/2 lb 4 oz rump or sirloin steak, cubed

2 large red peppers, deseeded and cut into small chunks

green and red lettuce leaves, to serve

Put the rice wine, soy sauce, hoisin sauce, garlic, chilli, ginger and spring onions in a large bowl and mix until well combined. Season to taste with salt and pepper.

Thread the meat onto 8 metal skewers, alternating with chunks of red pepper, leaving a small space at either end.

Transfer the skewers to the bowl and turn to coat in the marinade. Cover and leave to marinate in the refrigerator for at least 2^1/$_2$ hours or overnight.

Preheat the barbecue. Remove the skewers from the marinade and cook over hot coals, turning frequently, for 10–15 minutes, or until the meat is cooked through.

Serve immediately on a bed of green and red lettuce leaves.

MEATBALLS ON STICKS

SERVES 8

4 pork and herb sausages

115 g/4 oz fresh beef mince

85 g/3 oz fresh white breadcrumbs

1 onion, finely chopped

2 tbsp chopped mixed fresh herbs, such as parsley, thyme and sage

1 egg, lightly beaten

salt and pepper

sunflower oil, for brushing

sauces of your choice, to serve

Preheat the barbecue. Remove the sausage meat from the skins of the sausages, put in a large bowl and break up with a fork. Add the beef mince, breadcrumbs, onion, herbs and egg. Season the mixture to taste with salt and pepper and stir well with a wooden spoon until thoroughly blended.

Shape the mixture into small balls, about the size of golf balls, between the palms of your hands. Spear each one with a wooden cocktail stick and brush with oil.

Cook over medium-hot coals, turning frequently and brushing with more oil as necessary, for 10 minutes, or until cooked through. Transfer to a large serving plate and serve immediately with a choice of sauces.

AN INCREASING NUMBER OF FLAVOURED SAUSAGES ARE AVAILABLE, FROM LEEK AND BLACK PEPPER TO CHILLI, AND CAN BE USED FOR THESE MEATBALLS.

9

ACCOMPANIMENTS

Meat benefits from numerous trimmings, from sauces and stuffings to vegetables and potatoes. Find out how to cook potatoes to crisp, golden perfection, or how to make Chestnut and Sausage Stuffing, Horseradish or Mint Sauce, or traditional gravies. A good marinade can transform an otherwise dull piece of meat into something quite extraordinary — check out the citrus and herb marinades or Honey Mustard Marinade for delicious combinations to tantalize your tastebuds.

APRICOT, HORSERADISH AND MINT SAUCES

To make the Apricot Sauce, put the apricots and syrup into a food processor or blender and process until smooth.

Pour the purée into a saucepan, add the other ingredients and mix together well. Heat over a low heat for 4–5 minutes until warm. Remove from the heat and pour into a serving jug. This sauce goes well with gammon.

To make the Quick Horseradish Sauce, mix the horseradish and crème fraîche together in a small bowl until well blended. Serve the sauce with roast beef.

To make the Mint Sauce, make sure that the mint is clean (if the mint is dirty, wash it gently and dry thoroughly) and tear the leaves from their stems.

Put the leaves on a chopping board and sprinkle with the sugar. Chop the leaves finely (the sugar helps the chopping process) and put in a small heatproof bowl. Pour over the boiling water and stir until the sugar has dissolved.

Stir in the vinegar, then cover and leave to stand for 30 minutes. This sauce goes particularly well with roast lamb.

SERVES 6

APRICOT SAUCE

400 g/14 oz canned apricot halves in syrup

150 ml/5 fl oz vegetable stock

125 ml/4 fl oz Marsala

$^1/_2$ tsp ground ginger

$^1/_2$ tsp ground cinnamon

salt and pepper

QUICK HORSERADISH SAUCE

6 tbsp creamed horseradish sauce

6 tbsp crème fraîche

MINT SAUCE

small bunch of fresh mint

2 tsp caster sugar

2 tbsp boiling water

2 tbsp white wine vinegar

CRANBERRY SAUCE

Cut the strips of lemon and orange rind into thin shreds and put in a heavy-based saucepan.

If using fresh cranberries, rinse well and remove any stalks. Add the cranberries, citrus juice and sugar to the saucepan and cook over a medium heat, stirring occasionally, for 5 minutes, or until the cranberries are beginning to burst.

Sieve the juice into a clean saucepan and reserve the cranberries. Stir the arrowroot mixture into the juice, then bring to the boil, stirring constantly, until the sauce is smooth and thickened. Remove from the heat and stir in the reserved cranberries.

Transfer the sauce to a bowl and leave to cool, then cover and chill in the refrigerator.

SERVES 8

thinly pared rind and juice of 1 lemon

thinly pared rind and juice of 1 orange

350 g/12 oz cranberries, thawed if frozen

140 g/5 oz caster sugar

2 tbsp arrowroot blended with 3 tbsp cold water

TRADITIONAL GRAVIES

To make the Chicken Gravy, blend the cornflour with the water in a jug, then stir into the juices in the roasting tin. Put the roasting tin over a low heat and cook, stirring, until thickened. Add more water, if necessary. Season to taste with salt and pepper.

To make the Beef Gravy, pour off most of the fat from the roasting tin, leaving behind the meat juices and the sediment. Put the roasting tin over a medium heat and scrape all the sediment from the base of the tin. Sprinkle in the flour and quickly mix it into the juices with a small whisk. When you have a smooth paste, gradually add the wine and most of the stock, whisking constantly. Bring to the boil, then reduce the heat to a gentle simmer and cook for 2–3 minutes. Season to taste with salt and pepper and add the remaining stock, if necessary, and a little Worcestershire sauce, if you like.

SERVES 4

CHICKEN GRAVY

1 tbsp cornflour

2 tbsp water

pan juices from a chicken roasting tin

salt and pepper

BEEF GRAVY

pan juices from a meat roasting tin

3 tbsp flour

300 ml/10 fl oz red wine

300 ml/10 fl oz beef stock

Worcestershire sauce (optional)

salt and pepper

MUSHROOM STUFFING

SERVES 6–8

55 g/2 oz butter

3 shallots, chopped

225 g/8 oz mixed wild and cultivated mushrooms, chopped

115 g/4 oz pork sausage meat

85 g/3 oz fresh white breadcrumbs

few drops of truffle oil (optional)

salt and pepper

Melt the butter in a heavy-based frying pan over a low heat. Add the shallots and cook, stirring occasionally, for 5 minutes, or until softened. Add the mushrooms and cook, stirring occasionally, until their juices have evaporated.

Transfer the shallots and mushrooms to a bowl, add the sausage meat, breadcrumbs and truffle oil, if using, and season to taste with salt and pepper. Mix together well.

If you are planning to stuff a turkey or goose, fill only the neck cavity. It is safer and more reliable to cook the stuffing separately, either rolled into small balls and put on a baking sheet or spooned into an ovenproof dish.

Cook the separate stuffing in a preheated oven at 190°C/375°F/Gas Mark 5 for 30–40 minutes. It should be allowed a longer cooking time if you are roasting a bird at a lower temperature in the same oven.

CHESTNUT AND SAUSAGE STUFFING

Mix the sausage meat and chestnut purée together in a bowl, then stir in the walnuts, apricots, parsley, chives and sage. Stir in enough of the cream to make a firm, but not dry, mixture. Season to taste with salt and pepper.

If you are planning to stuff a turkey or goose, fill only the neck cavity. It is safer and more reliable to cook the stuffing separately, either rolled into small balls and put on a baking sheet, or spooned into an ovenproof dish.

Cook the separate stuffing in a preheated oven at 190°C/375°F/Gas Mark 5 for 30–40 minutes. It should be allowed a longer cooking time if you are roasting a bird at a lower temperature in the same oven.

SERVES 6–8

225 g/8 oz pork sausage meat

225 g/8 oz unsweetened chestnut purée

85 g/3 oz shelled walnuts, chopped

115 g/4 oz ready-to-eat dried apricots, chopped

2 tbsp chopped fresh parsley

2 tbsp snipped fresh chives

2 tsp chopped fresh sage

4–5 tbsp double cream

salt and pepper

CITRUS AND HERB MARINADES

ORANGE AND MARJORAM

1 orange

125 ml/4 fl oz olive oil

4 tbsp dry white wine

4 tbsp white wine vinegar

1 tbsp snipped fresh chives

1 tbsp chopped fresh marjoram

salt and pepper

THAI-SPICED LIME

1 lemon grass stalk

finely grated rind and juice of 1 lime

4 tbsp sesame oil

2 tbsp light soy sauce

pinch of ground ginger

1 tbsp chopped fresh coriander

salt and pepper

BASIL AND LEMON

finely grated rind of 1 lemon

4 tbsp lemon juice

1 tbsp balsamic vinegar

2 tbsp red wine vinegar

2 tbsp virgin olive oil

1 tbsp chopped fresh oregano

1 tbsp chopped fresh basil

salt and pepper

To make the Orange and Marjoram Marinade, remove the rind from the orange with a zester, or grate it finely, then squeeze the juice.

Mix the orange rind and juice with all the remaining ingredients in a small, non-metallic bowl, whisking together to combine.

To make the Thai-spiced Lime Marinade, bruise the lemon grass by crushing it with a rolling pin. Mix all the remaining ingredients together in a small, non-metallic bowl, then mix in the lemon grass.

To make the Basil and Lemon Marinade, whisk all the ingredients together in a small, non-metallic bowl. Keep the marinades covered with clingfilm or store in screw-top jars in the refrigerator, ready for using as marinades or bastes.

HONEY MUSTARD MARINADE

Mix all the ingredients, except the oil, together in a small bowl.

Gradually add the oil, whisking constantly, until it is fully absorbed into the mixture.

Use to marinate and baste chicken or pork, especially spare ribs.

2 tbsp clear honey

2 tbsp wholegrain mustard

1 tsp ground ginger

1 tsp garlic powder

2 tsp finely chopped
fresh rosemary

4 tbsp dark soy sauce

50 ml/2 fl oz olive oil

MINTED YOGURT MARINADE

Crush the garlic with the salt on a chopping board to make a paste. Scrape into a bowl and stir in the mint, yogurt and cumin, if using.

If you are using the onion, put it in a food processor, together with the yogurt mixture, and process for a few seconds, or until the mixture is coarsely blended.

Use to marinate and baste lamb. Garnish with mint leaves.

2 garlic cloves, crushed

1 tsp salt

4 tbsp finely chopped fresh mint

225 ml/8 fl oz natural yogurt

1 tsp ground cumin, coriander seeds or ground cinnamon (optional)

1 onion, roughly chopped (optional)

a few mint leaves, to garnish

ROAST SUMMER VEGETABLES

SERVES 4

2 tbsp olive oil

1 fennel bulb

2 red onions

2 beef tomatoes

1 aubergine

2 courgettes

1 yellow pepper

1 red pepper

1 orange pepper

4 garlic cloves, peeled

4 fresh rosemary sprigs

pepper

Preheat the oven to 200°C/400°F/ Gas Mark 6.

Brush a large ovenproof dish with a little of the oil. Cut the fennel bulb, onions and tomatoes into wedges. Slice the aubergine and courgettes thickly, then deseed all the peppers and cut into chunks. Arrange the vegetables in the dish and tuck the garlic cloves and rosemary sprigs among them. Drizzle with the remaining oil and season to taste with pepper.

Roast the vegetables in the preheated oven for 20–25 minutes, or until tender and beginning to turn golden brown. Turn the vegetables over halfway through the cooking time.

Serve the vegetables straight from the dish or transfer them to a warmed serving plate. Serve as an accompaniment to barbecued or grilled meat and poultry.

ROASTING BRINGS OUT THE FULL FLAVOUR AND SWEETNESS OF THE PEPPERS, AUBERGINES, COURGETTES AND ONIONS.

ROAST ROOT VEGETABLES

SERVES 4–6

3 parsnips, peeled and cut into 5-cm/2-inch pieces

4 baby turnips, quartered

3 carrots, peeled and cut into 5-cm/2-inch pieces

450 g/1 lb butternut squash, peeled and cut into 5-cm/2-inch chunks

450 g/1 lb sweet potato, peeled and cut into 5-cm/2-inch chunks

2 garlic cloves, finely chopped

2 tbsp chopped fresh rosemary

2 tbsp chopped fresh thyme

2 tsp chopped fresh sage

3 tbsp olive oil

salt and pepper

2 tbsp chopped fresh mixed herbs, such as parsley, thyme and mint, to garnish

Preheat the oven to 220°C/425°F/Gas Mark 7.

Arrange all the vegetables in a single layer in a large roasting tin. Scatter over the garlic and the chopped herbs.

Pour over the oil and season well with the salt and pepper.

Toss all the ingredients together until well mixed and coated with the oil (you can leave them to marinate at this stage to allow the flavours to be absorbed).

Roast the vegetables at the top of the preheated oven for 50–60 minutes until tender and well browned. Turn the vegetables over halfway through the cooking time.

Sprinkle with the mixed herbs to garnish and add a final sprinkling of salt and pepper. Serve with roast meat, poultry and game.

SHALLOTS OR WEDGES OF RED ONION CAN BE ADDED TO THE ROOT VEGETABLES TO GIVE ADDITIONAL FLAVOUR AND TEXTURE. WHOLE CLOVES OF UNPEELED GARLIC ARE ALSO GOOD ROASTED WITH THE OTHER VEGETABLES. YOU CAN THEN SQUEEZE OUT THE CREAMY COOKED GARLIC OVER THE VEGETABLES WHEN EATING THEM.

ROAST POTATOES

Preheat the oven to 220°C/425°F/ Gas Mark 7.

Cook the potatoes in a large saucepan of boiling salted water over a medium heat, covered, for 5–7 minutes. They will still be firm. Remove from the heat.

Meanwhile, put the dripping in a roasting tin and put in the preheated oven to heat.

Drain the potatoes well and return to the saucepan. Cover with the lid and firmly shake the saucepan so that the surface of the potatoes is roughened.

Remove the roasting tin from the oven and carefully tip the potatoes into the hot dripping. Baste until well coated with the dripping.

Roast the potatoes at the top of the preheated oven for 45–50 minutes until browned all over and thoroughly crisp. Turn the potatoes over and baste again only once halfway through the cooking time, otherwise the crunchy edges will be destroyed.

Carefully transfer the potatoes from the roasting tin to a warmed serving dish. Sprinkle with a little salt and serve immediately. Any leftovers are delicious cold.

Serve with roast or grilled meat, poultry and game.

SERVES 6

1.3 kg/3 lb large floury potatoes, such as King Edwards, Maris Piper or Desirée, peeled and cut into even-sized chunks

3 tbsp beef dripping, goose fat, duck fat or olive oil

salt

PERFECT MASH

Peel the potatoes, putting them in cold water as you prepare the remainder to prevent them from turning brown.

Cut the potatoes into even-sized chunks and cook in a large saucepan of boiling salted water over a medium heat, covered, for 20–25 minutes until tender. Test with the point of a knife, but do make sure that you test right to the middle to avoid lumps.

Remove the saucepan from the heat and drain the potatoes. Return the potatoes to the hot saucepan and mash with a potato masher until smooth.

Add the butter and continue to mash until it is thoroughly incorporated, then add the hot milk (it is better hot because the potatoes absorb it more quickly to produce a creamier mash).

Season to taste with salt and pepper and serve immediately as an accompaniment to thick casseroles, braised dishes or grilled meat and poultry.

SERVES 4

900 g/2 lb floury potatoes, such as King Edwards, Maris Piper or Desirée

55 g/2 oz butter

3 tbsp hot milk

salt and pepper

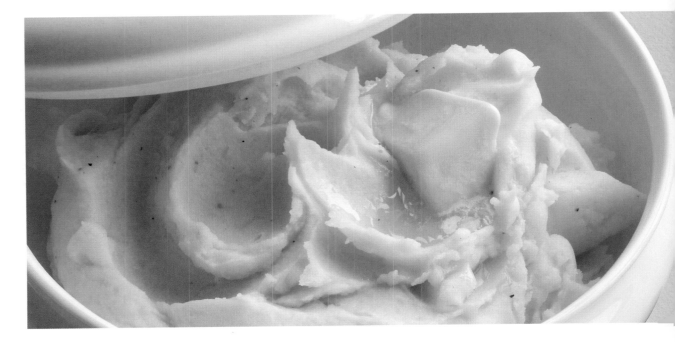

INDEX